THE ACTOR'S GUIDE TO SUCCESS…

…. GET THE JOB, GET THE LIFE.

BY MICHAELA LONGDEN

Copyright © 2023

All rights reserved. No part of this publication may be reproduced, distributed, or transmitted in any form or by any means, including photocopying, recording, or other electronic or mechanical methods, without the prior written permission of the publisher, except in the case of brief quotations embodied in critical reviews and certain other noncommercial uses permitted by copyright law.

Book Design by Aeyshaa

ISBN: 978-1-83556-042-6

CONTENTS

INTRODUCTION	5
A BRIEF HISTORY	10
01. Acting Technique – The Toolbook Section	**24**
1. Script Analysis: Understanding the Script	25
2. The Themes	31
3. Relationships.	35
4. Environment	39
5. Imagination, CGI, and Green Screens	42
6. Environment and the Bigger Picture	46
7. The Circumstances	49
8. Finding an Objective	57
9. Actions and the "How"	73
10. Actioning in Practice	87
11. Learning Your Script	90
12. Finding the Emotion	92
13. Listening, Intuition, and Instinct	103
14. Imagination	115
15. Human Psychology	123
16. Improvisation	125
17. Commitment	128
18. Vulnerability	133

19. Professionalism	136
20. Attitude	140
21. Auditions	143
22. The Techniques Concluded	147

02. Creating A Powerful Mindset — 149

1. Mindfulness, Focus, and Distractions	152
2. Meditation	160
3. Self-Trust	167
4. Nerves, Self-Belief, and Courage	172
5. Visualisation	180
6. Fear	186
7. Fear of the Future	190
8. Silence	194
9. Negative self-talk and limiting beliefs	199
10. Positivity and Motivation	219
11. Goal Setting and Achieving Clarity	224
12. Compassion to YOU	232
13. Gratitude	234

CONCLUSION — 237
BIBLIOGRAPHY — 241

INTRODUCTION

This book aims to share with you the techniques, lessons, and mindset that I have learnt and developed during my time as an actress, life coach, and acting coach over the past decade. Acting, like this book, is not for the faint-hearted. You will need to work hard, listen tenaciously, and practice mindfully. If you're up for the challenge, strap yourself in, and enjoy the ride.

So, you want to work as an actor. Do you? Do you *really*? Do you even know what an actor does in their day-to-day? This book will provide insight into:

1. What the life of an actor really looks like.
2. Useful acting techniques and technological advances that should inform your craft.
3. How to achieve a powerful actor's mindset.
4. Some important lessons that I have learnt along the way during my career.

Many of the practitioners we study, such as Lee Strasberg, Sanford Meisner, Konstantin Stanislavski, and Stella Adler, have inspirational acting technique insights that are fundamental to informing any actor's craft. However, these practitioners' theories were formed during a very different time in terms of technology. The way we watch actors and consume performances has changed since then. Whilst people still attend the theatre, more people today experience an actor's work in their own homes or at the cinema, watching on huge screens where you can see every wrinkle, every strand of hair, and every subtle movement. The early 2000s saw a rise in the use of CGI, green screens, and special effects, and the rapid improvement in digital and camera advancements has meant the way we make films has changed forever. Films are now created in higher definition, often using a multiple-camera set-up (numerous cameras filming all at once from different angles), and the editorial suite has become the saving grace of most on-the-day mishaps.

The industry has also become much more competitive. The acting profession is unregulated, meaning anyone can be an actor with no formal credentials required. In some ways, this is a positive shift, as it opens the acting industry to people from all walks of life and backgrounds. Acting, which was previously seen as a profession for the elite, is now open to everyone. Additionally, the rise of reality television stars and influencers has meant that film investors sometimes compromise talent for blue ticks to encourage higher viewing numbers.

Competition for viewers is now tougher than ever, with multiple streaming services offering television on demand; therefore, it has become imperative that producers and investors take action to ensure a project's success. Often, to guarantee viewers, the reality-show famous will appear on stage and television as the desperate need for a "known person" to fill the role often becomes more important than an individual's talent. We live in an age where everyone wants to be famous, and perhaps only a fair few have a genuine interest in becoming an actor. With more people chasing fame, rejection is increasingly common, competition is tougher, and the life of an actor is more emotionally and mentally vexing. In a world where talent can be overlooked for popularity and *who* you know seemingly matters more than *what* you know, actors must work harder than ever to stay ahead of the game. If we are to survive this wonderful but transformed industry, we must give power to both our technique *and* our mindset.

I have noticed that whilst there are many great acting technique books, there are very few that discuss how a healthy mindset contributes to an individual's success. Mindset is equally, if not more so, important than technique. If an actor has a great mindset and their technique is okay, they may still get the job. At the audition, they will be confident, engaging, and they will collaborate professionally and positively with the casting director. However, if an actor has a brilliant technique but a bad mindset, no matter how good of an actor they may be in the rehearsal room, things are likely to fail in the audition room. An individual with an untrained mindset may self-sabotage any attempts to move their career forward, especially if they have limiting beliefs regarding what is possible for them. Fear becomes their enemy: fear of getting it wrong, not being good enough, looking the fool, or sometimes even fear of success itself.

When we experience fear, the pre-frontal cortex (the part of our brain responsible for reasoning, judgement, and working memory) is compromised. This occurs due to an amygdala hijack. The amygdala part of the brain is responsible for processing our emotions, and when we feel we are in danger, it activates the fight, flight, or freeze response. The result? Basic functions such as our working memory, impulses, and coherent speech are compromised. This is an absolute disaster for actors, who require all of these skills to carry out their work effectively. Consequences for an actor are likely to include forgetting lines, stuttering, speech incoherence, and an inability to listen properly or take directions well.

From the early stages of my teaching career, I saw some of the most talented students crumble under pressure, and students who had arguably less talent thrive. I felt frustrated that it didn't matter how much some individuals prepared or how much they perfected their technique; if their mindset was poor and they believed, perhaps unconsciously, that they would fail, guess what happened? They failed. For those of you who have studied the power of the subconscious mind, you will be aware of how integral our subconscious mind is to everything we do in life, including our decision-making. It is, therefore, essential that we consider not only what we consume in terms of our body for good health but also in terms of our minds. It surprises me how many individuals are extremely focused on what they eat to remain externally healthy but equally neglect their internal mental health. As the body and mind are intrinsically interlinked, wouldn't it be beneficial to work on both of these areas?

Having a healthy mindset *and* a healthy body will affect everything we do. Our bodies give us the vessel, and our mind gives us the inspired action. If we are to thrive, we must take ownership of developing a sound mind, paying particular attention to the things that we consume, what we read, what we listen to, the people we hang around with, and the media we absorb. All of these things have an effect on the way we think – which ultimately controls all aspects of our lives. Yes, that's right, EVERYTHING. Your environment and your subconscious beliefs, in my opinion, are the two most important things that you will need to shape in order to have a successful career. Most of our thoughts are subconscious; they run automatically and often stem from our subconscious beliefs. A belief in basic terms is an acceptance that something is true. These beliefs rule our behaviours. What we truly believe and what we surround ourselves with will shape everything that we are and everything we become.

The acting profession is filled with opportunities and rejections. The latter is, unfortunately, predominant for most people. Therefore, we need to take ownership of creating a productive mindset and perspective so that we see rejection as a learning curve and an opportunity, not as a failure. Perspective shifts are essential if we are to create a long-lasting, happy acting career, and surely, that is the goal. For those of you who lack patience and expect quick success, you must be mindful of the difficult expectations you are placing on yourself. You may be working hard in this industry to no avail for one year or maybe even thirty. The point is, are you willing to go the whole way? To power through regardless of how long it takes? In an industry where talent, luck, the right place, and the right time all matter, there are some elements you cannot control and trying to do so will only result in disappointment.

This book will start with a brief overview of my history, followed by some powerful acting techniques I have learnt along the way, and we will conclude with a discussion about mindset strategies. Please use this book in the way that best serves you. Skip chapters where necessary and use those that apply as a toolkit throughout your career. Each section includes tasks that will aid you on your journey. I advise that you use these to your advantage, and I hope this toolkit helps you moving forward.

A BRIEF HISTORY

I was raised single-handedly by my mum and was one of two daughters. My father was an abusive alcoholic and, when I was three years old, he left our family home situated on a council estate in Chesterfield. My older sister was reserved, enjoyed reading, and was the solitary sort; however, I was full of energy and loved to entertain people. Growing up, I always knew that I wanted to be a performer. I had bright ginger hair and whenever we had guests around at the house, my mum would ask me to sing *Annie*, and I was more than happy to oblige. I often would have a "happy half an hour" where I was giddy and would goof around in front of our guests and play "the performer". I loved it; this was how I got love, acceptance, and attention. I thrived off it. So did my mum.

My mum's big smile encouraged me, and I became convinced that I was destined to become the next Celine Dion or Geri Halliwell. This was all well and good until I realised that perhaps my talents were not naturally in music performance. As much as I loved singing and showcasing my dance routines to whoever would watch, I quickly realised that I didn't pick up routines quickly and my singing voice needed a lot of work. I soon recognised that no amount of training would turn me into the newest member of the Spice Girls. I guess that was my first life lesson.

✏️ **Lesson One: To succeed, it is important to understand your limitations and carefully select which ones can be improved upon.**

This lesson taught me I could still enjoy singing and dancing, but perhaps I should do so in an isolated arena where no feet could get trampled on. As I aged, I moved past this dream and started focusing on acting, something I was more naturally gifted in. Now, let me clarify, I do not believe that things cannot be worked on. Natural talent is only half of a success story; courage, determination, and consistency make up the other. However, I realised that understanding my own limitations would save me a lot of time and future heartache.

So, there I was, a young kid living in poverty wanting to make a name for herself in the world of showbiz. I immersed myself in films and TV soaps and making it as an actress became my goal. As a family, we never went to the theatre because money was tight; however, we would sit together on a Sunday and watch long, classic films, and I would watch the actors and actresses with awe. I gradually became interested in screen acting, but I had my doubts. As a child, I was very logical and realistic (the two words that will always hold any dreamer from living their potential). Life was tough for my family, and I often thought, *Is this career suitable for a poor kid like me? Am I good enough? Do I deserve it?*

✏️ **Lesson Two: Lead with love (always)**

In primary school, I was never picked for Mary in the nativity play; I was always a Shepherd or a sheep. I was also never the "pretty kid" at school – actually, I was quite the opposite. I had the brightest ginger hair and Deidre Barlow glasses (for those of you too young, a character in Coronation Street who wore the most unattractive glasses). I was scrawny, geeky, and wore hand-me-downs. I never saw myself as someone who could win a leading role. Despite this, I had a burning desire to act.

My mum used to say I was quite sensitive as a child, which was derived from my ability to empathise with others. I've always been able to place myself naturally in others' shoes and see things from their perspective. Even in school, when I was called names because of my red hair and glasses, I could never insult those same people back; I'd felt the insult's sting and didn't want to inflict that on another. This was the same with the characters that I watched on screen. Whenever I picked up a script or watched a film, I became engrossed in the character's life. I felt their pain and their struggles. I was obsessed with other people and their lives. I wanted to understand their story, but, more importantly, I wanted to be the one to tell it. So, in my first year of secondary school, I decided to apply for a role in Romeo and Juliet – my first casting.

This was a big step for me, though I didn't apply for Juliet. Of course, I would have loved to have played that role, but my fear of rejection and of being judged for even trying prevented me from taking that kind of silly action. So, I instead applied for a smaller role, and I got it! The opening night was nerve-wracking, but I enjoyed every moment of it. Being on stage and entertaining an audience . . . I felt alive. I was in love.

✎ Lesson Three: Lean into fear. You might just enjoy it.

Unfortunately, the older I got, the more practical and logical my opinions became. I worked hard academically and started to believe that acting was a hobby but never a career to pursue unless I wanted to continue a life in poverty. I lived in fear of this future so never spoke about my dreams of being an actor and tried my hardest to suppress them.

In my late teens, I continued to appear in school plays, never applying for the lead, of course, and when it came to choosing my GCSEs, I decided to take Drama. This subject was my favourite. I loved my teacher, and I loved the lessons. In Drama, I could escape being me for a while and become someone else. Most actors have one moment where everything changed, and this was mine. In class, we were set the task to write and perform our own monologue. I was very excited! I gave my woman a narrative; she was a woman haunted by the death of her child. I rigorously planned all the things I wanted to incorporate into the performance. I carefully considered the lighting, the music, and the props. I wanted the audience to feel uneasy, so I used candlelight. This lighting would bring a gothic atmosphere – perfect! I wanted the music to be chilling, so I chose Evanescence, a rock band at the time who played moody and haunting music. My dialogue was written to be disoriented to reflect the woman's despair. I also made sure there was a crescendo, a moment of climax which would shock the audience.

The day arrived to showcase our monologues. I went first. I was nervous, and as I got up to light the candles and set the stage, my hands started to sweat. I lay down on the floor, taking my first position as the woman. Then, I took a deep breath and began. I loved every minute and for the entirety of the performance, I felt as though I were in a dream. Post-performance, I was in a haze – I had lost all sense of where I was. I felt like I had awakened from a past life. I'll never forget the shocked faces I was greeted with when I came to myself and looked around at the end of the performance.

In all honesty, I had zoned out during the performance. I couldn't remember an awful lot of it. I knew there were moments where I was completely immersed, moments of real terror, and, to my horror, I was almost certain I had screamed at one point. I gave my audience solid eye-contact and worked the room better than a sales executive at a networking event. I was in the zone, present and alive. I moved with the feelings of my character and connected with all my senses, committing wholeheartedly to the performance and the story that my character so desperately needed to tell. I was in a flow state, fearless. It was this moment that would change the rest of my life.

When I sat down, my classmates smiled and said how wonderful they thought my performance was. I smiled with joy at the feedback and took to my chair eagerly waiting to watch my classmates' performances. However, as the next person got up to perform, and the person after that, something strange happened. I began to feel very silly. No one else had used music, props, or lighting. Dear God, no one else screamed! I was a fish out of water, the black swan, and I stood out. I started to feel embarrassed. I thought of my peers' smiles and wondered whether they really enjoyed my performance or whether they just humoured me. Were they judging me? Did they think I was a fool and laugh *at* me rather than smile *with* me? I convinced myself that my classmates thought my performance was stupid, dishonest, and ridiculous. I convinced myself that they smiled out of pity and their shocked faces marked expressions of horror. I wanted the floor to swallow me whole. I spent the rest of that lesson feeling incredibly anxious and regretful that I had interpreted it all wrong.

 Lesson Four: Surely, lesson four was… don't take stupid risks???

At the end of the lesson, the teacher congratulated us all. She reiterated how brave we all were at the age of fifteen to get up on stage and write and deliver a monologue. She then looked me in the eyes and individually congratulated me for creating something so watchable, which incorporated so many different aspects of storytelling. I smiled at her, and as I looked around, not one of my classmates was looking at me judgementally. Not one of them looked horrified. None of them were laughing at me. They were all smiling.

After class, many of my peers came up to me and said that they felt embarrassed to show their performance after mine. I couldn't believe it; they were embarrassed for not being more creative. At that moment it dawned on me that the embarrassment I had felt hadn't come from anyone other than myself. It was my own projections about my own insecurities that had consumed me. My insecurities about being different and standing out for the wrong reasons. Insecurities concerning my self-worth, my place in the acting world, and whether I was just too weird-looking. I had never been "normal". I had always stood out in many ways. But what I didn't realise was these differences gave me a uniqueness that would ultimately aid my success in the years to come.

✏️ Actual Lesson Four: Take risks, be brave, and lean into fear.

I continued to study Drama at A-level and I went on to study a BA in Drama and Theatre Studies at Liverpool Hope University. I did apply to one Drama School in Manchester but I didn't prepare for the audition. Instead, I self-sabotaged and left everything to the last minute. The audition was probably the worst acting experience of my life. A lack of preparation meant my nerves were uncontrollable and I forgot all of my lines. Embarrassed and ashamed, I convinced myself that I was never going to be good enough and that I would be a teacher and not an actor. I was so scared of rejection and people thinking that I was stupid to have that dream, and I had an overwhelming fear of not being good enough. So, off I went to become "a teacher". University was a ball; however, I didn't enjoy the course at all – it was all theory and not much acting. I was disappointed and still clinging to the hope of being an actress, so I secretly started to look for acting jobs.

I didn't tell anyone else, and I didn't know where to start. At a complete loss, I applied for a graduate scheme in management in a lovely restaurant called Nando's instead. I had worked there part-time during university, and it seemed like a "safe" thing to do. There were eight thousand applicants and eight places, and I was lucky enough to get one. The managers were just as shocked as I was when they heard the news; I wasn't the most diligent staff member. I often went to work hungover and spent most of my shift talking or with my head over the toilet. I was a real classy Nandoca (Nando's term for a waitress). However, on the assessment days, my competitive nature kicked in and I wanted to win. I knew that I was academically strong and believed I could win. Within a few months, I'd relocated to Manchester to start the job.

 Lesson Five: What you believe you are capable of becomes your reality.

My time in management at Nando's was relatively short-lived, eighteen months in total. Whilst I was good at the job, the hours were long and unsociable, looking after a team made me anxious, and the thought of this being my life forever became unbearable. I couldn't shake my desire to act and so after a nightmare of a shift, I decided something needed to change. The fear of staying where I was and of living in regret forced me to take action on my dream. I started to look for any auditions I could find in Manchester. Paid, unpaid, it didn't matter to me. I just wanted to try. Within weeks, I was cast in a fringe play and a short film. I was unbelievably excited. The first day on set came and I was a nervous wreck – how could I, Michaela Longden, be filming? I couldn't actually believe it. I mentioned before that there are moments that change the course of your life, and the events that transpired on that set changed mine forever. On that set, I met my first-ever acting agent. This agent was also an actor and just so happened to have been cast in the film. When he asked if I was seeking representation and if I would contact him, I nearly weed myself! I was in complete disbelief. My first short unpaid film landed me my first agent. For the first time, I felt validated. This made me reconsider my position at Nando's and what I wanted from life. What are the chances of landing an acting agent from your first job? *Slim*, I thought. I believed this was a sign. After so many years of repressing my desire, I finally accepted that I wanted to be an actress.

Lesson Six: What you resist persists. Don't waste time waiting for external validation to start!

The deadline for the only northern Drama School I wanted to attend, ALRA, was in five days. I applied. *Shit*, I thought. *Five days to remember two monologues. Not again!* Was history repeating itself? I had five days to get ready and prepare and I was working full-time, sixty-hour weeks at Nando's. Even if I did by some miracle get in, I would then have six months to source fifteen grand. *Crap*!

Lesson Seven: Lean into OPPORTUNITY and consider the HOW later.

The day of the audition came, and I wasn't as nervous as I thought I would be. I had already acquired my acting agent and I was professionally auditioning. The week before, I had nervously auditioned for my first-ever commercial. The casting director had asked me to do my best Naomi Campbell strut, and in my confusion of what that entailed, I tripped up over a light stand. Surely this wouldn't go as bad as that? Also, I knew I didn't have the money for the school, so I guess this was just to see whether I could get in. That was the story I told myself. As usual, the self-sabotage kicked in and I got lost on the way there. I arrived at the audition, sweating, with my top on back to front and a few minutes late. *Calm down*, I told myself. *This is a no-pressure event because I can't afford to go anyway!*

As requested, I partook in some physical workshops and performed my two monologues. One was Emilia from *Othello*, feisty and outspoken; she was true to my casting type. The other, however, was the character Ben from a play called *Lion in the Streets*. Ben was definitely not my casting type, but I loved the script, and it was short, so I went with my gut and did it anyway. At the audition, I saw a lot of talented actresses and actors and I felt like the black sheep in the room, an imposter. The last stage was the interview stage. As I walked into the room to meet my interviewer, he looked at me and asked, "Can you afford this?" I looked at him and confidently said, "No." He smiled and thanked me for coming. I left the room and as I walked out, I smiled. Something inside me said that my life was about to change. BINGO. I got in, and I got in with a *full effing scholarship*! I was ecstatic.

✎ Lesson Eight: Let go of chasing an OUTCOME and enjoy the ride.

Drama School was tough but I learnt a lot and I graduated with an amazing new agent. I booked a main house theatre tour within a few months and was getting some fantastic auditions, but still, deep down, I didn't really believe I could win and suffered badly with my nerves. Everyone was validating my skill, everyone except for the person who really mattered, me. Most of us have self-limiting beliefs that restrain us and mean we self-sabotage; some we are aware of and others we bury. These beliefs can debilitate us, stagnate us, and stop us from pursuing what we truly desire. These beliefs can make us doubt ourselves and other people. They can make us feel judged and they can make us judge others. Many of these beliefs start from an early age; mine certainly did.

Getting into Drama School wasn't the final hurdle I needed to jump over to become a successful actress. At auditions, I would look around the room and feel that everyone else was more deserving to be there than I was. They had more money; they didn't grow up on a council estate fearful of their mum not making the rent; they were better looking; they had better agents and probably already knew the casting director. My focus was entirely on what I thought everyone else had and everything that I lacked. My focus was on the stories that I had made up inside my own head. I was nervous, insecure, and lacked confidence and charisma in the room. I forgot my lines, didn't listen or collaborate, and was overwhelmingly fearful. I approached my characters with caution, always careful not to play the role too big in case I embarrassed myself. I'd forgotten all about Lesson Four – being brave and taking risks. I was overly concerned with what others thought rather than my intuition and instinct. I wasn't involved and I wasn't collaborating; I was judgemental and overly critical of myself and my craft. I projected my own insecurities outwards and in turn, I stopped bringing ideas to the table and standing out. The more rejection I received, the more fearful I became. I didn't trust myself, so no one else did either.

In my late twenties, I got into an abusive relationship which left me a total mess. I was anxious, depressed, and suffering from insomnia and PTSD. I had let someone cross so many boundaries and I didn't know who I was anymore. I felt completely lost and so ashamed of what had happened. After trying to mask my feelings with alcohol and distractions, I soon realised that enough was enough. My mental health was on the decline, and I couldn't take it any longer. It was time to fight for my life. I took responsibility for my life and decided it was time to make changes. It became imperative that I worked on my self-esteem, my boundaries, my self-image, and my limiting beliefs. I was determined to come out of this mess stronger than ever, knowing myself better than ever.

I journaled consistently and spent hours and hours working through my past. I dissected my traumas and I sought to understand my triggers and bad habits. I learnt the tools to monitor my thoughts and understand my body's alarm signals so that I could work through my fears and insecurities. I realised that my lack of self-love meant that I often gave readily and freely, even if I compromised myself in the process. My desire to feel accepted, loved, validated, and helpful to others made me a perfect victim. But not anymore. At that point, I chose to take control of my life and beliefs. I read for three hours a day about mindset and psychology. I was deliberate with what I fed my body and my mind. I released judgement, replaced hate with forgiveness, anger with love, and I learnt how to reconnect with myself with compassion.

At twenty-eight, I had a significant breakthrough when I spoke to a life coach. She told me that in comparison with many other actors, I had been relatively successful. I was making money doing what I loved. She then asked me why I thought that was. I remember saying that my success was pure luck, but that nothing had come from this success because people "like me" would always find it hard to do well in this profession. She then asked what I meant by "people like me". At that moment, I realised I held a belief that my background and upbringing controlled my fate. I believed that I would always find it difficult to succeed as an actor because I grew up poor and ugly. I innately believed that I was not good enough, unworthy, and that any attention I got (romantically or professionally) wasn't deserved. My self-image of who I was and what I thought I was capable of didn't line up with who I wanted to be and who I was, in fact, becoming. I had unearthed an unconscious belief responsible for many blockages during my life. These blockages in my early career manifested in many ways: self-sabotage, running away from opportunities, comparisons, self-doubt, always feeling inferior, avoidance, and failure. FEAR ruled EVERYTHING!

 Lesson Nine: Your past does not equal your future. Become aware of your blockages, projections, and limiting beliefs. Become aware of what makes you fearful.

The years I'd spent neglecting my emotional mind, past traumas, and insecurities had caught up with me. We can very easily focus on what we don't have and on others' opinions in this industry. If you step outside of these expectations and remove other people from the equation, you will realise that deep down, the only thing standing in the way of your success is yourself. No one's opinions will make or destroy you as quickly as the ones you create yourself. What you think of yourself paves the way for what others think of you. A person who holds undeniable self-respect carries themselves in a certain way. A person who is comfortable in their own skin behaves in a certain way. A person who believes in themselves creates success over and over again. Over the last decade, I have dedicated a vast amount of time and energy to mastering how to create a powerful mindset. A mindset that encourages growth, possibilities, and positive change. One that leans into fear and listens to intuition. One that expands rather than contracts. One that empowers and is responsible for a peak performance state. Over the years my commitment to my mindset has meant that the nerves have gone, the fear has gone, and the judgement has gone. But more than that, my mindset has made me believe that anything is possible. I have built a happy life as an actor, with a successful coaching business that I adore, where I help others achieve empowerment. I have bought my own home, written this book, and appeared in films that have been released worldwide. I no longer fear auditions but thrive in them. I lean into opportunities, and I act for ME, not for anyone else! I continue to work hard at my mindset and my craft because it makes me feel incredible, and feeling incredible is addictive. This book was written to help you learn acting techniques to inform your craft and the mindset techniques that will inform your way of life, encouraging a journey into self-love and self-acceptance. This book was written to give you more than just an acting lesson but a mindset shift. One that I hope will change your life for the better forever. You must understand, however, that this work doesn't stop when you close this book. Ultimately, your success and progression lie within you.

Lesson Ten: Continue to stretch, learn, and grow. You will never look back.

Now, I ask the question again: *Do you really want to be an actor?* I'm not referring to whether you want fame, money, status, or lifestyle. I'm talking about whether you also want everything in-between: the consistent auditions, the continuous learning and growth, the rejections, the fatigue, the last-minute castings, the cancelled holidays, the forever fighting and forever aspiring, the highs and the lows, the self-esteem battles, the jobs on the side, the excitement and exhilaration, the energy to make the required mindset shifts, the self-tapes, the uncertainty, the battle through fear, the failures and the wins, the missed celebrations, the long hours, the extreme filming conditions, the chaos, the financial instability, the "Oh, I was so close", the time, the commitment, the dedication, the thick skin, and the real dream. If you answered yes, read on!

The acting industry is wonderful, exhilarating, and never the same two days in a row, but it is not normal. You must work hard, show up, and get involved. You must learn your craft and own who you are to ensure you have the best chance of landing a role. You must look after your body and your mind, understand your brand, and not take anything personally. To truly fall in love with acting, you must learn to fall in love with yourself, accepting everything you are and all that you are not. You must love not only the end goal, but what you are physically, emotionally, and mentally about to embark on. You must learn to love the process and manage your expectations but never hold yourself back.

This book will ask certain things of you. It will ask you to look inwards and seek honest answers that may be holding you back. It is not a guarantee to quick success. Nothing ever is. But it is my hope that this book will help you become a more resilient, successful, and, most importantly, happier actor. In my opinion, persistence is key, and we can only persist if we enjoy the journey. Happy reading.

PART 1.

ACTING TECHNIQUE – THE TOOLBOOK SECTION

Welcome to the Technique Toolbook Section. This part of the book will give you some of the main tools to help you break down a script. Each heading will include tasks to help you implement and cement your learning. It's completely up to you how long you spend on each section, so utilise this part of the book as needed.

I would like to reiterate that this book is for all stages of acting development, so there may be sections you want to skim over if you have worked on your technique for some time. The script analysis section below is designed as a guide for all levels, so please use it in the way most useful to you. Many of these techniques have been inspired by the work of Stanislavski, Lee Strasberg, Sanford Meisner and Uta Hagen. Useful resources include Stanislavski's *An Actor Prepares,* Nick Moseley's *Actioning and how to do it,* Sanford Meisner On Acting, and Uta Hagen's *Respect for Acting and A Challenge* for the Actor.

1. Script Analysis: Understanding the Script

Script analysis is essential for any actor, but what is script analysis? It is simply understanding the script on a deeper level. If we are to portray a character realistically with all their nuances and layers, we must understand everything about their world. It surprises me how many actors I meet who do not facilitate script analysis into their preparation. They lift the lines off the page immediately, getting it on its feet before they have even fully understood what's happening. These actors forget to ask key questions that will inform their practice. Stanislavski's approach states there are seven key questions you should first ask:

1. Who am I?
2. Where am I?
3. What time is it?
4. What do I want?
5. Why do I want it?
6. How will I get it?
7. What do I need to overcome?

The above questions will aid your understanding of the script and are useful to keep in mind. Every well-written scene should move the narrative in some way to propel the storyline and characters forward, and as actors, we need to understand this. Most full scripts will give you most of the details that you need to know about your character and the world they live in. However, on some occasions, you will not be given the whole script. There are a variety of reasons for this, mostly to do with confidentiality or the script being incomplete. Usually, you will be given a synopsis of the plot and your character, however, if no other materials are available (this may happen on a script-on-arrival audition), it is our job as actors to fill in the gaps.

First things first. Read the script.

TASK

1. Read the script once.
2. Read the script twice.
3. Read it again a third time.

What Is Happening?

Reading through the scene thoroughly is important. If the actor neglects this, they run the risk of missing important narrative clues and shifts in tensions such as the climactic moment within the scene. The climactic moment is the moment of no return; a moment in the script where everything changes. To uncover the "what", we need to consider the following: what do you understand from the script? What is happening based on facts? Where do things change?

The scene below (Script 1) will be used throughout the script analysis section of this book. Please refer to it as and when you need to. Let's use it now and establish the "what".

SCRIPT 1.

One: Hi.

Two: Hiya.

One: Where have you been?

Two: Out.

One: I got that. I'm asking where?

Two: Do you want anything else?

One: Can I see you later?

Two: No.

What's happening in this scene? Let's look at the facts. Understanding the facts will give us strong guidelines to formulate a narrative.

What Are the Facts?

So, what are facts? Facts are things that we know to be true as there is evidence in the script to back them up. Facts allow us to place the scene and afford us clarity. One example of a fact could be that it is morning. Other facts could be the age of your character, their marital status, or where they live. Remember that a fact is something the script supports as truth. Facts give us firm context and allow us to make good character choices that are backed by the writer's vision.

So, from this Script 1, we understand that the facts are:

- Two has been out.
- Two refuses to see One later.
- One has asked to see Two.
- One quizzed Two about their whereabouts.
- The sentences are short and snappy.

Using the facts, we can start to make some strong presumptions of what is going on in the script. It's highly likely that there has been tension between the two characters given the avoidant language and short, snappy sentences. It is important to note here that the language used and the sentence structure can inform the actor of their character's feelings at a particular time.

Based on our limited facts and understanding in this particular scene, we could decide that Two has had an argument with One and is angry at them. This would explain the abrupt and sharp answers and their reluctance to cooperate with One. If we accept this decision and adhere to it when we read the script again, we will see the script with new eyes and hear it with new ears. Our read is not just bound by the lines on the page, it now embraces a specific story and circumstance. "What is happening?" must be the first question answered in any given scene and finding out the facts is often a good start to this process. We must always know *why* our character is there and *what* is going on in the scene if we are ever going to portray them realistically. Think of it like this: can you commit openly and fully to the action in the scene if you do not know what the action is or what your character's motives are?

TASK

1. What are the facts in the scene?
2. What action moves the story along? What's actually happening? If you don't know, make an educated guess.

What Don't We Know?

Whilst facts establish what we know, they also highlight what we need to find out.

If we look at Script 1 again, there are a lot of things we do not know, so we must start to make assumptions. However, it's important not to overcomplicate things, especially if we are short on time. What are the significant unknowns that may dramatically alter your performance and understanding of the script?

For example, the below unknowns in Script 1 could change the dynamic between the characters significantly:

- What is the relationship between the characters? Are they in a romantic relationship? Are they family, acquaintances, or in a friendship?

- What happened to cause the argument? Infidelity? Or did one eat the other's Mars bar? Both of these would offer a very different scene.
- Where is this conversation happening?
- What time is it?
- How long have they known one another?
- Where has Two been?

These are only a few examples of the unknowns in this particular scene, and I would recommend that you add more to your own process. If we are to fully understand our characters' intentions, journey, and thought processes in the scene, we must make some interesting, educated decisions that are backed by the script. The best choices will be those that add intensity and gravitas to the scene, but these must run linear with the author's intentions if we are to deliver an authentic and non-jarring performance. Too often, actors make decisions based on their desire to "show" some sort of emotion or they overcomplicate their decisions. Perhaps they believe this will add more excitement to their performance. Usually, however, it leaves the audience (and the actor) feeling rather confused.

An actor's desire for a memorable performance can interfere with their ability to tell the story truthfully. We must remember that actors are players to the script; we are storytellers. An actor's job is to tell the story with integrity and honesty. Making a decision that does not correlate with the writing will be your biggest mistake. We are all guilty of wanting to create material that showcases our ability; however, we must always remember that we are hired to serve the story and not our ego. Remember any decisions you make MUST be backed up by the script. Once you have your options, then you can consider the one that offers you the most stake. Think of stake like leverage. What does your character have to gain or lose? Always consider what's at stake for your character and whether you need to make a decision to use a higher stake to create a more charged performance. For example, if there has been an infidelity and you have children the stake is much higher than if you do not. This rise in stake will create a more emotionally charged performance.

So, let's use educated guesses to answer some unknowns in Script 1.

- **What is their relationship?** Answer: Romantic. The characters seem to live with each other, so it makes sense that it could be a romantic relationship.
- **What happened to cause the argument?** Answer: Accusations of infidelity. The argument could be about anything, but this choice encourages higher stakes, pace, and energy. The "stake" is the term to describe what the character has to lose.
- **Where are they?** Answer: At home. The question "Where have you been?" Could suggest that they are at home.
- **What time is it?** Answer: Late one evening. It doesn't say, but a later time adds more stake to Character One in the scene.
- **How long have they known one another?** Answer: Five years. The longer the relationship, the more they have to lose.

If you read Script 1 again with these unknowns implemented, the read will change, natural pauses or "beats" will ensue, and a new character attitude will be created. This underpins the deeper contextual meaning behind the story. These new layers will create a performance with more emotional depth and a stronger subtext, meaning the story that takes place "between the lines". For example, a man and his wife wake up after a heavy argument. The man asks the woman if she's okay. The woman replies yes, but her eyes and her demeanour say no. This is a clear example of subtext. It is not something directly spoken or said, but something felt by the audience and characters.

It's important that we fill in any gaps because we should know every detail about our characters' lives; however, we can only work with the material we're given to prepare from, so don't worry if what you use to fill any gaps is found out to be wrong later. If we were given Script 1 for an audition, the casting director would expect you to make some choices. Don't worry about making wrong choices, worry about making *good* choices.

Good choices are educated, interesting, and stem from the facts. They are solid and backed by the script, have high stakes for the character, and create intrigue for the audience.

TASK

1. Write down what you don't know about the scene.
2. Fill in the gaps by making educated guesses.

2. The Themes

Once you have established the facts and filled in any unanswered questions, the next step is understanding what is at the heart of the script. What is the script's dominant message? Furthermore, what is really at the heart of this scene for your character? What is the challenge they face? The best way to think about this is to explore the script's theme. Usually, there is not just one theme in any given script, there are multiple. For example, in the film *How to Be Single* there are many different themes, including love, loss, and identity. We can even take it one step further and establish the overriding theme, which in this example is "learning to love yourself".

Most themes are very evident in the script, especially if we're working with a full text; however, if the script is vague and we're unaware of the theme, we must make some more decisions. Let's look back to our work with Script 1. We've already made some educated guesses that can inform our reading of the scene's themes, such as infidelity, loss, jealousy, and fear. Understanding these themes allows us to consider the pace, life, and energy of the piece. A scene with a theme of lost love and jealousy may have long silences or interrupted speech; it will have high tension points and create a feeling of uneasiness. Conversely, a scene with a theme of "love conquers all" would have a fluid pace and be energetic but light, warm, and grounded. Being aware of the theme will affect the delivery of our performance, as the theme can highlight a more appropriate rhythm and tone.

Whilst it's useful to note the themes and explore them, we must be sure we do not "play" them. Actors should never play an emotional state such as "fearful" or "jealous". Themes can often highlight certain emotions within the scene, and although it's important that we understand the emotions our characters are feeling, they should not be the sole focus of the scene. The consequences can be a one-dimensional performance with no journey or energy. We will discuss this further in later topics but for now, understand that a script's theme lets us explore it in more depth. The theme is not something we play, but something that informs us of the overarching topic, rhythm, pace, and tone. It is the heart of the script.

TASK

1. Determine your script's theme.

Now you have your theme, take a moment to really think about what it means to you. Have you ever experienced anything related to your theme? Taking the theme "infidelity", have you ever been a victim or guilty of this? Our job as an actor isn't just portraying a character's story, it's about relating to them in every way and empathising with their situation. It's about connection and a deeper understanding of their emotional and internal conflicts. Emotional conflict is where a character may be experiencing two or more emotions that do not coincide with each other. For example, the theme of newfound love could bring butterflies and excitement to the character, but they could also experience fear and anxiety as they start to feel more vulnerable. Internal conflict is where there is a conflict in what we desire or what we believe. For example, we want answers, but deep down we don't want to know the truth. We want to lose weight, but we don't believe we can be slim (so we eat the doughnut).

Explore your themes with depth, and don't accept surface-layer answers.

TASK

1. Determine the themes present in the script.
2. Write about these themes and what they mean to you.
3. Recall memories, past events, films, music, art, and people that remind you of this theme.
4. Consider the theme and the emotional conflicts that commonly occur within it. The theme of "loss" could carry conflicting emotions of "fear" and "relief". We fear loss but perhaps can also be relieved by it.

Once you have explored aspects of this theme and what it means to you, link it back to what is happening in the actual scene. Let's go back to Script 1 again.

Script 1.

One: Hi

Two: Hiya

One: Where have you been?

Two: Out.

One: I got that. I'm asking where?

Two: Do you want anything else?

One: Can I see you later?

Two: No.

We previously agreed Two is convinced that One is cheating on them. One is cheating on them.. The main theme may be "deception" but other themes such as love, loss, jealousy, hate, desperation, loyalty, and fear also could be present. Uncovering various themes will allow us to understand what feelings, beliefs, and desires our characters may be experiencing. I often encourage my students to look for opposing themes and experiment with them to unearth internal conflicts in the scene. For example, Script 1 could harbour opposing themes of love and hate. Perhaps Two hates One for their apparent infidelity but also loves them deeply and can't imagine a life without them. Most actors will focus on the hate aspect, but if we additionally explore love we can perhaps find moments in which we see Two's very conflicting trains of thought. This enriches our performance and adds vulnerability, and we avoid making cliches. Understanding the themes in a scene allows us to truly observe the writer's intentions, therefore providing answers to why our characters behave in the way that they do.

TASK

1. Consider what your character's internal and emotional conflicts are. Internal conflict is where they are in conflict with what they believe or want, and emotional conflict is where two opposing emotions are running simultaneously.

Once you have outlined the different themes within the script, try summarising the main thought driving your character through the scene in one line. Examples include "leave me alone", "listen to me", and "tell me the truth". The line could be anything, but it's important that you can connect to its meaning.

In our example scene, One's line could be "I'm sorry", and Two's could be "don't come near me".

TASK

1. Write your overarching thought at the top of your script.
2. Read and perform the scene and let this line inform every word you say.

3. Relationships.

Hold tight, people, because this chapter is an important one. We need to understand not only *who* is in the scene but *why* we are interacting with them and our attitude towards them. Understanding the "who" is usually very obvious, as this is generally stated or suggested within the script. Your relationship could be, for example, a family member, a work colleague, or a love interest. However, there are rare occasions in which relationships are unclear, and you will need to ask for the answer or make an educated guess.

TASK

1. Write down each character mentioned in the script.
2. Write down their relationship to you i.e., brother, friend, mother, etc.
3. Write down any other characters that are never mentioned but may be important to you, such as parents.

Once we have noted any relationships, we must delve deeper by analysing our emotional connection with these other characters. Do we like them? What evidence is there to suggest that we do or don't? Is there any conflict between the characters? Is there evidence to suggest there has been some sort of bigger conflict previously? How do we speak to them? What do we say about them? What do they say about us? This research will enable us to generate a deeper understanding of how we feel towards other people within the scene.

Humans and their relationships are complex and are impacted by the past. In life, we never have only a single view of a person. Just because people are family members does not necessarily mean we treat them stereotypically as family. My sister once said to me, "You are the only person who knows how to make me go crazy." My sister and I have a very close relationship, but apparently, I know which buttons to press to wind her up. We often allow the people we love to have power over our emotions. We generate an attitude, energy, and feeling towards a significant person based on the experiences we've had with them. Experiences where strong emotions of pain arose change our relationships with people the most. The brain clings onto the memories formed from these emotions so that we learn and avoid them again in the future.

Take this example: in a scene, we are introduced to two sisters. The sisters are talking about a party for their mother's birthday. The dialogue seems pleasant, but we are aware from a previous interaction that one sister actually resents the other for their success and always being the "golden child". The resented sister is aware of this bitterness and often tries to downplay her success as she craves acceptance. If the actors implement this knowledge into the scene, allowing it to change the delivery and pace, the audience will start to notice the cracks in this relationship.

TASK

1. Write down your views and opinions about the characters within your script based on the facts and then fill in any gaps you do not know.

2. Consider any conflicting emotions you hold towards the characters in the scene and the possible reasons for this.

Many actors skip this important part of script analysis. They note down any relationships and consider their relationship research complete. I've known of actors who haven't even discussed relationships before filming – this is an absolute no-no! Relationship analysis is crucial in winning or realistically portraying a role. This is what separates the novices from the experts. Experts understand that all writing is based on interactions and relationships with people, places, and objects. If we do not research the relationships in depth, the audience misses half of the story and will struggle to relate to it. It is the intricacies of the relationships that help the audience relate to the characters. The audience will understand the scope of the relationships through the way a character reacts, touches, speaks, or engages with another character. These details assist in creating a well-rounded story, enabling the audience to understand why characters behave the way they do. Without this nuance and detail, the audience will disengage.

At this point, it is also crucial to consider a character's status. Status is defined by how important or respected an individual is or how much power they hold in relation to someone else. A high-status character could be an upper class, privileged male who works as a lawyer, for example, whereas a lower-status character could be a female cleaner who works in a train station. However, when the lawyer speaks with a king, he becomes the lower-status character and when the cleaner speaks with a homeless person, she gains the higher status. Therefore, our status is entirely reliant on the individuals we're with and our specific connection to them. In addition to understanding their interpersonal relationships, it is crucial to understand how our character perceives their own status in relation to others. Do they consider themselves to have a higher, similar, or lower status? Understanding this will give us valuable insights into our character's behaviour, speech, and mannerisms when interacting with the different people in their lives. Humans exhibit distinct responses based on the person they are interacting with, and within each conversation lies a struggle for status. How you conduct yourself with your boss will be different to your behaviour with your friend. Sometimes, the balance of status in a relationship is harmonious, characterised by a mutual exchange and generosity. This type of dynamic is typically found in friendships. On the other hand, other status battles are more ferocious. These clashes are commonly observed in strained or stretched relationships, or in situations where there is contention for power and authority.

To clearly see moments of conflict or tension within a scene, I recommend that my students mark which character has the higher status in each line and note where their character gives it or takes it away. It also gives you greater insights into the characters' relationships. For instance, if you presumed that two characters were friends but notice that one is constantly placing their status higher than the other, consider what this tells you about their relationship. It could be that one character is harbouring underlying resentment or jealousy or sees their friend as beneath them. If that is the case, perhaps this friendship isn't a friendship at all.

TASK

1. Look at the relationships in your script. Can you relate to these? Draw upon past experiences in your life. When have you experienced a relationship like this? If your character is in love with another in the scene, draw upon a time you were in love. How did it feel?

2. If you cannot relate to the relationship, can you consider a time that you felt a similar feeling toward another? For instance, take this scene: a stranger threatens you in the street and forces you to give them your phone. In reality, you've never been robbed by a stranger, so have no direct basis of comparison. However, perhaps you have felt threatened by

someone and thought they might hurt you. Use your similar experiences to inform your relationship choices.

3. If you still struggle to connect to the relationship, put yourself in your character's shoes. Imagine their life and the other character and consider how you would feel about this other person. Close your eyes so you can really concentrate on generating a feeling.

4. Consider the opposite. Usually, we have the ability to hate those we love, so if you're playing a person who's in love, think of a time when the character you're in love with hurt you.

5. Consider the status battle. Who holds higher status? When do you lose or gain it?

So, you have completed your work on relationships, right? Wrong! Most actors only focus on the relationship that their characters have with other people, but relationships are also created with our environment and the world around us. We all have opinions about our environment and what it means to us. We all behave differently in certain environments. Some of us love to hike in the outdoors whilst others prefer a film by the fire. Some people love to travel whilst others prefer routine and home. We change our behaviours and interactions in different environments. We also change our attitude, pace, and energy. Therefore, it becomes fundamental that actors explore this further.

4. Environment

Our character's behaviour will be influenced by their environment. If our character is familiar with their environment, they will behave very differently to when the environment is unfamiliar. The same is true for safe vs dangerous environments and public vs private ones. For instance, consider this scene: Tom and

Mary are arguing about the fact he never does the dishes, and it always makes them late.

How could their environment change the way they communicate during this exchange? If they're in a private environment at home, it would be safe and familiar enough for them to reveal their "worst self" with no inhibitions or fears of others watching them. This familiarity would allow the characters to raise their voices significantly louder, pace, and slam doors because they don't need to be worried about "making a scene". However, if the scene unfolds in a public setting, things would change considerably. If your character is aware of the presence of others who could potentially witness or hear the unfolding events, it is reasonable to expect different behaviour. An altercation between a couple during a church sermon would differ from one occurring in their own home or at a friend's dinner party.

To effectively portray your character, consider these key questions: where are we? Do we feel comfortable? Is it a safe space? What is our history with this environment? Have we been here before? Are we familiar with the people present? Is there a chance of someone overhearing? Do you care about the opinions of potential listeners? Reflecting on these factors will enable you to make more nuanced choices regarding your character's behaviours and interactions. As actors, it is essential to consider the environment as it influences every aspect of our character's communication, thereby aiding the depiction of the story's world. We must consider how the environment affects the volume of our character's voice, the social norms they adhere to, and their level of comfort or discomfort in expressing themselves within their current surroundings. Do they casually put their feet up or do they appear rigid and awkward? The environment permeates everything, from their posture and gestures to their speech and overall attitude toward the world around them.

TASK

1. Write down where your character is during the scene. What is your environment?
2. Are they alone? Is anyone else with them? Can anyone else overhear them speaking?
3. Do they currently feel safe or threatened? Would they normally feel at ease but feel uncomfortable due to the scene's setting? For instance, a character may ordinarily feel comfortable in their parents' house but not when having an argument with their spouse. Consider how the environment changes their behaviour.

When considering our environment, it's crucial to make strong character choices and stick to them. Every character is unique and will respond differently based on their attitude and personal history. Some characters may take more "risks" or exhibit unexpected behaviours in specific environments, just as it happens in real life. We've all seen couples fighting in public or heard of an abusive relationship where the abuser seemed so charming to the outside world. We might have come across individuals shouting rude comments at supermarket staff or overheard neighbours arguing from our gardens. Whilst understanding how the environment affects our behaviour is crucial, we must also understand our character's attitude and persona. Are they the kind of person who lets the environment dictate their behaviour? Do they even care?

Do not underestimate your character. Sometimes, opting for the obvious choice isn't the best decision. If you're playing a character who does not abide by the rules, consider exploring this aspect further during your rehearsals. Great outcomes can emerge from the unexpected.

TASK

1. Remember, not everyone adheres to the same social graces, so it's important to consider all the possibilities for your character. Some individuals are happy to argue in public whilst others despise it. Similarly, some people are happy to be affectionate in public, whilst others prefer not to. Where does your character stand on these matters? Utilise the information, make educated decisions, and trust your instincts to guide your choices.

5. Imagination, CGI, and Green Screens

In my first few years as an actor, I performed a scene set in a club. When filming in a loud environment, dialogue is recorded in silence for the boom operator to capture, with sound added in post-production. This scene involved an argument, and I was raring to go. I entered into the scene, crossed the dancefloor to my "ex-boyfriend" and started delivering my lines in a very passionate and argumentative way only to be stopped by the word "CUT!"

The director looked at me and said, "You need to shout." I looked at him, confused. He continued, "You're in a club. There would be music, and you would be shouting." I immediately felt very stupid, as I had overlooked this obvious detail in the script. Well, not entirely. I knew it was set in a club, but somehow, the absence of actual music made this fact slip my mind. I hadn't truly considered how the environment would impact my character's voice, choices, movements, and the need to compensate for the loud music. If the director hadn't caught my mistake, the scene would have looked pretty unconvincing. This was a learning curve for me, as I became very aware of how the environment can entirely transform your entire delivery.

Similarly, you must also consider what your character can see. We live in an age where the use of CGI and green screens are all too common, meaning the actors on set often can't see everything that will appear in the final film, as these elements are added in post-production. The same applies when acting with animals or babies; they are often removed from the scene ("cheated") for noise and continuity purposes. Continuity refers to maintaining chronological consistency in the action portrayed. Typically, there is a person on set dedicated to ensuring that the scene remains coherent and matches in the editing process. For instance, if a character is seen drinking during a specific line, they must consistently drink whenever that line is spoken to ensure coherence across shots and takes.

When filming, the term "shot" describes the continuation of frames, which are still images captured by the camera. These frames differ in proximity to the subject (the main focus in the shot) and the chosen angle. One example of a shot could be a close-up of someone's eyes from the left. A "take" refers to the repeated recording of a particular shot. Usually there will be multiple takes of a shot as it is very rare that the shot is perfect the first time. There may be sound issues, lighting issues or continuity issues that need resolving. Continuity errors must be avoided for the scene to make sense and appear believable. The final edit typically combines the best takes of individual shots to create a scene, so it is imperative that these scenes cut together seamlessly. Maintaining continuity can be problematic when the scene involves elements that are difficult to control, such as babies, the weather, animals, and any other unpredictable subjects. The director may wish to change the angle where possible to cheat these elements out of the frame, ensuring they remain unseen, or shoot indoors to prevent continuity issues with weather and lighting. The absence of these missing objects, people, and visuals means actors need to activate their imagination further.

One of my first professional roles was playing Ellie in a low-budget feature film titled *The Creature Below*. In this film, Ellie had multiple scenes working alongside "the creature". In one scene, the creature had brutally ripped my sister apart and was now poised to come after me whilst I was helplessly tied to a radiator. My character was obviously terrified and desperate to escape. Traumatised and chained to a radiator, she had no hope. The scene was set in a cold, damp basement in Ellie's sister's house; however, this environment was also the creature's home. The director explained that he would be filming from behind the creature so it's tentacles would "dirty the frame", meaning that the tentacle would appear in the shot but not be in focus.

Now, the creature wasn't CGI, so I had an eye-line focus. However, it did not look intimidating or scary. Not at all. What I had to work with was a huge, purple polystyrene ball smothered in some kind of lubricant to give it a sheen. Oh, and my co-actor and very good friend Dan was manipulating its polystyrene tentacles from behind. Going into that scene, I understood that I needed to tap into my imagination to deliver an honest performance; however, at times, all I wanted to do was laugh. Whilst Dan's manipulation of the tentacles was magnificent, it was also hilarious. Often, we work with elements that bear no resemblance to their final appearance in the edited film. In reality, the situation may inspire an entirely different reaction (like laughter). However, we must remain true to the story and the character at all times. Whenever you get the giggles or are reminded of the production process, close your eyes, and take a minute. Ignite your imagination and take yourself to the place of your character, to the world they are in, and breathe.

Game of Thrones and *Lord of the Rings* are perfect examples of cases when actors needed to use their imaginations to tell the story effectively. Both productions include otherworldly environments and creatures such as dragons, giants, and Orks. Whilst practical effects may have been used on some of these projects,

I imagine CGI played a major role in creating most of the effects, especially the dragons. Practical effects refer to physical creations, like a werewolf head and body, which offer actors a visual reference. When CGI is used actors must rely entirely on their imagination and commitment. Actor commitment is essential and is the result of unwavering confidence and fearlessness. The self-conscious actor struggles to commit fully for fear of being judged. When actors fully commit, they give wholeheartedly to the scene and produce memorable performances.

In the sci-fi short film *Terminal*, much of the work involved green screens, as the story was set in a dystopian future where the world had experienced global changes. One particular scene was set on a balcony situated in one of the most elite buildings in the world. The balcony was high up, among skyscrapers and futuristic aircrafts. It represented the world of *Terminal*, a new world, one very different from our own. For my character, it felt familiar and yet unfamiliar, grand yet unappreciated and unwelcome. In reality, the balcony was at a university in Leeds, with a rather gloomy and unimpressive surrounding. Green screens were used to cover the gloomy sights of Leeds so that CGI could be used later. It was my job to realistically convince the audience that my added surroundings were very much real. I needed to visualise with clarity the world of *Terminal* whilst simultaneously embracing the internal conflict my character now felt towards her changed world. This might not seem too difficult, however, with lengthy scripts, problematic weather conditions, potential nerves, and food as props, all of a sudden, it can feel like the actor has a lot to think about. If, however, we prepare for this beforehand, we can navigate this process much easier, anticipating any problems that may arise.

TASK

1. Consider these questions: will music be added in post-production but absent whilst filming? Will CGI be used? Will

you work with a green screen? What will you need to imagine that will not be there when filming?
2. What is your character's attitude towards this environment? Is there any internal conflict?

6. Environment and the Bigger Picture

We take on characters from all walks of life, some of whom exist in worlds that are extremely dissimilar to our own. There are characters who live in spaceships, the future, the past, and displaced environments. To play these roles convincingly, we must explore the relationships between the character and the larger world in depth.

A good example is *The Hunger Games*, where Katniss becomes entangled in a deadly game in which twenty-four children and teenagers must fight until one remains. The game is set in a forest, and it would be easy to assume that Katniss only feels hate and fear towards this setting. However, in earlier scenes, we see how much Katniss loves the forest; it is her refuge and her safe space, where she is a great hunter and resides to seek peace. The forest within the Hunger Games, however, is a simulation, filled with dangers that contradict the familiarity. Katniss now faces an internal conflict in this environment. Her innate love and familiarity for the forest rivals the hate she has for the Games. To survive, she must adapt. As an actor, you can explore this new dynamic with her environment by portraying moments when Katniss feels the warmth and love for the forest and times where she feels desperation and fear, creating a more interesting character filled with colour and conflict.

When examining your own character's environment and world, I recommend writing down your personal feelings towards it and remember your thoughts during every scene.

TASK

Consider the following:

- What do you think about your character's environment? Do you have any conflicting thoughts? For example, is the environment a safe space because it's your home but also a fearful place because you're a domestic abuse victim?
- How does the environment and the elements or people within it make you feel?
- How does the environment change your character's behaviour in the scene?
- Is the setting familiar or unfamiliar?
- Are you in a public or private space?
- Is the environment hot or cold?

Specific choices are required to activate our imagination fully. This is especially important when in the audition room and during a self-tape, where there is no set or other characters or props. It is essential that you harness your imagination effectively to convince the audience that what they see is real. If you do this well, the audience will accept anything you present. Consider this audition scenario: you're playing the character Hayley, who has been placed inside a spaceship (unknowingly) and sent to Mars. In the scene where she wakes up for the first time and is met with her new environment, you must use whatever you have at your disposal to recreate the world of the story. Your voice, senses, costume, and every aspect of your delivery should contribute to its believability. What does your character see? What do they feel? What can they hear? Can you imagine it and be specific? Specificity will land you the role. Casting directors and directors will give the part to the actor who makes them FEEL immersed in the film or play's world.

At this point, we must become aware of our eye-lines. An eye-line refers where your eyes are focused. Each person or object referenced in the script requires a specific eye-line. Your eye-line tells the story of the scene, revealing the placement of everyone and everything. Inconsistencies in eye-lines quickly make the audience aware that the actor is acting. If you're on set, the director can help you as certain eye-lines may be required for the shot. Whilst working through your script, be aware and highlight any elements or characters that require specific eye-lines. This clarity will set you apart from other actors, especially in self-tapes. Most actors become so obsessed with the lines in the script that they forget the finer and crucial details that enable the audience to believe.

Always remember, we are storytellers. Be bold and assertive with your decisions whilst remaining true to the script and the author's intentions. One final note on this topic: although we seek detail and active imaginations, be careful not to "over distract" yourself with too much detail. Actors can easily become preoccupied and invest excessive energy in aspects that have no connection to the story or dramatic action of the scene, resulting in a confusing and overcomplicated performance. Make clear, confident choices but avoid getting too caught up in very minor details.

TASK

1. Using any given scene, consider the following questions and record your responses in character using a voice recorder or your phone.
    - Where are you?
    - What can you see? Be specific, is there a door? Windows? Is there light?
    - What can you feel?
    - What can you hear, smell, or even taste?

- Who is with you?
- Where are they standing? How do you feel about them?
- If you are alone, how do you feel about that?
- Is this place familiar to you?
- How long have you been here?

2. Once you have recorded this. Lie or sit down and close your eyes and listen to the recording. Take yourself into the world of the script. Run this exercise two or three more times if you feel you need greater clarity.

7. The Circumstances

Those of you who have received some actor training will most likely have come across Stanislavski's concept of the "Given Circumstance". The Given Circumstance encompasses everything we know about our character and the world they live in at that moment in time. It essentially answers the following questions: who are they? What is happening? Where are they? How did it take place? When is it happening? Why is this conversation happening? By asking these key questions, we can understand the character's current situation and the dynamics at play within the scene which allows us to make informed decisions. For example, how would a working-class male living in the 1920s behave differently to one living in the 1990s? How would the monarchy in the 1600s differ from our modern-day monarchy in the twenty-first century? It is equally important to consider the social, economic, and political contexts as they influence our character's behaviour and social graces. I always recommend writing down the key specifics of your character's Given Circumstance so that it's clear in your mind.

TASK

1. Write down your character's Given Circumstance, including the who, what, where, how, why, and when.
2. Note down the political, social, and historical contexts of the script.

The Previous Circumstance. What Has Gone Before?

Every character has a past; they didn't simply appear in the scene out of nowhere. They had life and prior experience. When we receive a script or a scene, we must consider what happened before. Even if we don't see or know the specifics, it still matters. Here's why. How often have you heard or said the words, "I am the way that I am because of something that happened in my past"? We are all shaped by our DNA (nature) and our past experiences (nurture). The past holds significant influence on who we are today, with all our quirks and flaws. Humans are filled with layers of learning acquired from past events. This knowledge shapes our beliefs and values. Combined with our perception, natural energy, and attitude, this knowledge forms our personality – a multidimensional one. Now, ask yourself: if we neglect a character's history, what do we risk losing when we portray them? The answer: everything. To convincingly portray our characters, we must understand how their past has shaped them and their beliefs. What has brought them to this point? We must consider this from two perspectives: the immediate previous circumstances and the historical background.

The immediate previous circumstance focuses on what occurred to the character shortly before the current scene and how this influences their arrival. How does the immediate previous circumstance resonate emotionally within them, and how does it shape their feelings about the current situation? For example, if your character had a heated argument with their partner in the previous scene and some time has passed, they might appear calmer and more inclined to speak in a composed manner, or perhaps they choose to remain silent. During rehearsals, explore different options to find what feels natural and aligns with the director's vision, then commit to it. Considering the immediate previous circumstance helps bring the appropriate energy and gravitas to the scene.

TASK

1. Write down the location or situation of your character in the immediate previous circumstance before the current scene. If you don't know, create a previous circumstance that connects with the known facts.

2. Using this information reflect on your character's emotional state as they enter the current scene. How do they feel internally at the beginning of the scene? Are they composed, resentful, calm, joyful, angry, or in love? Make a specific choice.

Understanding the previous circumstance is crucial during filming. When the call sheet is sent out (a document containing the shooting day's schedule for the cast and crew), you may notice that scenes aren't shot in chronological order. Shooting schedules often prioritise grouping scenes based on location, which facilitates transportation, lighting, and setting up the scene, as these tasks consume most of the time. Therefore, it's essential to remember your character's immediate preceding situation to ensure continuity and coherence in your performance. I recommend writing down this information at the top of your script as a reminder of the past events, enabling your present action to flow seamlessly from the previous scene. Additionally, it's crucial to note your emotional state after filming scenes, especially when filming takes place over an extended period and out of chronological order. This will help you maintain consistent energy, pace, and tone in the scenes to follow. Inconsistencies, such as transitioning from crying in one shot to being completely fine in the next (if there has been no time shifts), can be jarring for the audience.

When filming *The Ghost Within*, we conducted pickups for the most emotional scene in the film three months later. Pickups involve capturing additional shots or re-shooting specific scenes after the initial filming has concluded. These pickup shots need to align with the original footage in all aspects, including the emotional intensity. Fortunately, the team were able to show me the pre-recorded material which allowed me to review my emotional intensity and line delivery. However, this may not always be the case, and there have been instances where pickups occurred months later, and I needed to work solely from memory. To ensure continuity, it's crucial to record or document any emotional moments experienced during filming for future reference. It's also useful to note any unexpected reactions or occurrences that took place during the shoot, such as unplanned tears or a moment of laughter and consult with the director and which take he will use.

Furthermore, physicality plays a significant role in maintaining continuity. For example, if your character has been running away from a monster and then finds a safe hiding place in the next scene, they may still exhibit signs of panting and tense body language. We must always remember our character's journey and thoroughly understand their physical and emotional progression. If you're unsure at any moment about this, speak to your director to establish a shared vision. Scenes are often not shot chronologically, and most people interpret things differently. Therefore, it helps to gain clarity on your character's emotional journey with the director. It's essential that you take full responsibility for ensuring clarity over your character journey. Communicate with the director and raise any questions or concerns at an appropriate time. If you don't, you may regret it later. I have experienced disappointment when watching my work back and observed continuity issues with emotional intensity. In one particular project one shot which had me in tears was cut with another shot where the tears were gone (only seconds had passed between shots). The reason: these shots were in the same scene but in different locations, which meant that they were filmed at the start and end of shooting schedule. The director had asked me to cry in one shot (the one filmed later) but in the previous shot had asked me to look numb (filmed five days before). The consequence, my performance had been compromised. However I learnt something BIG: always establish a shared vision of the character's emotional turbulence in EACH scene BEFORE shooting. With this clarity, I could have ensured that I was in the right emotional state for both shots. I also learnt to take full responsibility over my character's emotional journey by remembering with clarity what was already filmed so that I could appropriately challenge the director if necessary. Remember, the director is watching not only your performance but also the lighting, shadows, background, and extras in the scene. Many factors need consideration, and sometimes, due to time restraints, certain aspects may be overlooked. However, maintaining a collaborative approach reduces the likelihood of such mistakes.

TASK

1. Write down the physical and emotional ranges your character may experience from scene to scene. Are you out of breath? Are you crying? Did you remove your wedding ring because of a recent separation? Are you limping due to a fall from a window? Be detailed, your performance depends on it. Some audience members love to pick out moments in films that don't "make sense". Let's make that near impossible.

The Historical Circumstance

The historical circumstance focuses on the character's broader background and history. It involves understanding their social and economic upbringing, which will help us define their social status and attitudes more clearly. Typically, you will receive information about your character's history when cast for a role. A small biography is often provided, highlighting crucial life moments that have shaped and impacted their life. The audition material usually contains this information, but if you feel that something important has been omitted and it could significantly impact your performance, you can try discussing it with the director or casting director beforehand, preferably via email through your agent. If that's not possible, you can always ask on the day of the audition or filming.

One suggestion I give to my students is to research the social, historical, and cultural aspects of the time period in which the characters grew up. Immerse yourself in that era. What were the popular toys of the time? Who was the political leader? What were the differences in laws and human rights? What did people do for fun? Were there any wars, pandemics, or major events? Consider how major events in your character's past have impacted who they are. This research will inform their manner of speaking and moving. Are they educated? Articulate? Do they have a distinct accent? The text itself usually provides valuable clues about a character's social status and class. Various key indicators, such as occupation, age, sex, wealth, and family position, help us understand a character's status. Status influences how they carry themselves, their speech, and their interactions with others. It also affects their own self-perception and their attitude towards those around them.

I recommend writing diary entries in character. This exercise proves particularly useful once you have secured the role and want to further your research. By writing these diary entries, you can create a visual history of your character and imagine what they have been through emotionally. It allows you to step into the shoes of the characters and truly consider what life is or was like for them. This exploration manifests in surprising ways. Suddenly, a specific room, setting, or prop carries a weight and significance that can completely transform your performance.

TASK

1. Determine your character's social status.

2. Research the social, economic, and historical context relevant to your character.

3. Write diary entries for your character, focusing on actions depicted in the script. For example, if your character returns to their family home where their sibling was murdered fifteen years ago, consider writing a diary entry expressing the conflicting emotions you would experience in this situation. These diary entries will greatly enhance your performance in these crucial scenes.

The Potential Future Circumstance

The next concept we need to explore is the potential future circumstance, which revolves around what could happen in the future. To grasp this concept, consider the hopes and fears of our characters before a given scene unfolds. Hopes and fears are the driving forces in our lives. All humans experience hope and fear on a daily basis, but it's often fear, not hope, that governs our lives. Fear, a fundamental survival instinct, arises from a lack of certainty or control. We seek certainty to feel safe and secure, but when it's absent, fear takes hold. Unfortunately, fear often stops us taking steps towards our burning desires by instilling doubt within us.

Our hopes and fears serve as powerful motivators that propel us into action. As humans, we are driven by our emotions, which are triggered by our desires and fears. Have you ever considered how you hope a future encounter with someone will unfold? Or perhaps contemplated the potential pitfalls? Our brains are wired to protect us from pain, so we naturally consider what could go wrong. When going on a date, we hope for a successful and enjoyable time, but we may fear rejection based on past experiences. This fear of rejection might deter us from taking action and mean we cancel the date instead. Similarly, in a job interview, we hope to make a good impression, yet we may fear inadequacy or unworthiness. These fears often lead to nervousness and anxiety, sabotaging our best efforts. We may hope for success but fear that we aren't capable, resulting in a state of "deliberation stagnation" where we fail to take necessary action to move ourselves forward. Understanding the hopes and fears of our characters allows us to understand their decisions and internal conflict. When examining a character's hopes and fears in a specific scene, always remember to look at previous scenes for a comprehensive understanding of the context.

Consider this scene: A and B are in a discussion. Previously, they had an argument about A spending too much time at work, with B feeling like A isn't prioritising their relationship. Both characters will undoubtedly have hopes and fears about their next meeting. A may fear that B will end the relationship, but they *hope* for a rational, conflict-free resolution. On the other hand, B may fear that A will spark another argument, but they *hope* that A will start to understand their reasons for working so hard. These "potential future circumstances" significantly impact the character's speech, movements, reactions, conflicts, and emotional states within any given scene. Hopes and fears provide clearer insights into our characters' motivations and reveal their vulnerability within a scene. Vulnerability arises when we see the frailties of a character, allowing the audience to relate because all humans have experienced feeling insecure, misunderstood, or fearful. This identification fosters a deeper understanding and care for the character, captivating the audience.

To deepen our exploration, let's examine our characters' hopes and fears on a broader scale, considering not only a single scene but their entire lives within the script. For example, let's take a character called Tom, who hopes to find love but has been scarred by immense pain in a past relationship, causing him to distance himself from any potential love interests and act like a cliche "player". When a new love interest enters the script, Tom's overwhelming fear leads him to behave in rather questionable ways. He blows hot and cold and treats the girl badly. Now, as an actor, you could simply label Tom as a player and leave that it at that, or you could explore Tom's hopes and fears, adding layers, subtext, and likability. Tom, deep down, wants and hopes to find love but fears that he will get hurt. Now Tom has character layers that allow the actor to tap into his unique vulnerabilities.

TASK

1. Considering the historical and current circumstances, reflect on your character's potential future circumstance. What are their hopes and fears for the scene, regardless of the script's outcome? What would be the consequences if their desired outcome wasn't achieved?

2. What does your character fear and hope for throughout the script?

8. Finding an Objective

The character's want is often referred to as their "objective". What your character wants in a scene may differ from their "hope". For example, a character on a first date may *hope* to find a true connection, but they may *want* a good dating experience. Hope is a deeper, underlying longing. One that lines up with the character's values and desires. The want is more immediate to that particular scene. Think of hope as a broader longing that takes time to fulfil, whereas want is something achievable within the scene.

Your character's objective in a scene is what propels them forward and drives your actions as an actor. It is a specific goal that you aim to achieve. Just like in real life, every character has an objective in each scene, driving their behaviour and interactions. Our actions in life are guided by intentions and objectives. For example, when we enter a cafe and order a drink, our objective is to satisfy our thirst or get a caffeine boost. This initial want prompts us to take action, bringing energy, momentum, and desire. We walk into the cafe, order our drink from the barista, and place our order to achieve our objective. As I write this book, my motivation stems from a want or objective to create a book that truly serves actors, helping them with their technique and mindset. Hopefully your desire in reading this book is to learn.

So, how do we uncover the want? Each character will have a different want in each scene. Within each scene we must explore what has happened to the character before and what is currently happening in this scene. What drives the story forward? In well-written scenes, there's often conflict, and as actors, we need to be aware of it. A writer wouldn't write a scene about Joe Blogs going to Cafe Nero to buy a coffee and spilling it on the floor unless it adds to the scene in some way. A scene exists to show something to the audience, to reveal part of the journey or expose a facet of the character. If Joe Bloggs goes to Cafe Nero to buy a coffee and accidentally spills it on the most beautiful girl he has ever seen, there's a story to be told. We must always consider why a scene is there and what purpose it serves because this informs us of what our characters want. When the Joe Bloggs bumps into the beautiful lady, his want has now shifted from wanting a coffee to wanting to talk to the beautiful lady. Objectives are typically aligned with your hopes and fears as these are the governing motives that drive us.

Now, let's apply all the previous script analysis to Script 2 and practise developing a specific, strong, and well-rounded objective.

The context for Script 2: A and B are having dinner. A has recently discovered that B has been messaging someone else, and A is convinced that B is having an affair.

Script 2

>A: Do you have anything to say?
>
>B: They were harmless messages.
>
>A: They were explicit messages.
>
>B: Oh, give it over. It was just a joke.
>
>A: Are you sure?
>
>B: Of course I am sure, what exactly are you accusing me of here?
>
>A: I think you know what I'm saying.
>
>B: There was nothing in those messages. It was harmless banter, but maybe you wouldn't understand that because you're too busy snooping through my phone!
>
>A: Yeah, with good right. Now you either tell me the truth or…
>
>B: Or what? I am telling you the truth. What do you want me to do? Shall we call him? Do you want me to call Dave?
>
>A: No.
>
>B: Because you know you are being irrational.

A: No, because he would never own up to it, would he? I just need you to tell me. If you're playing me for a fool, I need you to tell me.

B: You're being stupid.

A: Don't call me that.

B: How could you think that I would do something like this to you? I love you. I would never hurt you.

BEAT.

You need to think about what just happened here, because if you want this, there needs to be trust involved.

B Goes to leave.

A: Where are you going?

B: I need to get out of here.

→ Implementing Script Analysis So Far

So, let's break down the scene using some of the things we have learnt thus far.

Facts

A and B are at dinner and are in a relationship. A has looked through B's phone. A has found some suggestive messages from third party Dave and is accusing B of cheating. B denies cheating. B leaves the conversation.

What is actually happening?

A and B are having a heated discussion about potential infidelity.

What Do We Not Know?

Since we don't have the rest of the script, there are several unknowns. If this were an audition scene with limited material, I would ask some further questions. Do we believe B is having an affair? When did A look through B's phone? Was it recently or some time ago? This information would inform the energy of the argument. Why did A look through B's phone? Do we think this has happened before? How long have the pair been together? Has their relationship been turbulent? What are their jobs? Do they have children? Does A have an inkling of who B might be having an affair with?

Make a Choice

When in doubt or unsure of what decisions to make, always choose the ones that align with the story and have higher risks or stakes attached to them. For example, if A and B have been together for five years, there is arguably more to lose than if the pair have been together for five months. Your decisions must always be backed up by the script and always make sure that you choose to care. A character who doesn't care is disengaging and lacks energy and drive. We always care, even if we don't care about our partner, we care about something, such as our ego or future. Let's revisit some of those unanswered questions and make decisions based on the script that hold significant stakes.

- **Q: Do we think B is having an affair?** A: Yes, they are acting evasive, which heightens the stakes and internal conflict from both parties.
- **Q: Why did A look through B's phone? Do we think this has happened before?** A: It hasn't been proven before, but B's recent odd behaviour prompted them to investigate.
- **Q: When did A look through B's phone?** A: A looked the night before whilst B was asleep, contemplating how to bring it up.

- **Q: How long have the pair been together?** A: five years.
- **Q: Has their relationship been turbulent?** A: Every relationship has its ups and downs. Theirs has been no different.
- **Q: Do they have children?** A: No, there's no mention or sign of children.
- **Q: Do they live together?** A: Yes, this seems likely.

What Are the Themes?

Jealousy, hate, love, fear, loss, jeopardy, trust, monogamy, infidelity, abandonment, not being good enough.

Environment

Since they share a home, we can assume the environment is safe, private, and familiar to both of them. As we can assume they have no other housemates and no children, they likely feel comfortable being themselves around each other.

Relationships

The scene portrays a romantic relationship between the characters. We have decided they have been together for five years and have experienced their ups and downs.

The Previous Circumstance of the Scene

The confrontation at the dinner table arises from A looking at B's phone and discovering evidence of potential infidelity. It is assumed that B left their phone unattended at some point – perhaps during the previous night.

Historical Previous Circumstance

We can assume the scene takes place in a contemporary time period where mobile phones are commonly used. Whilst the class and educational background is unknown, we can have flexibility with our choices such as A being a teacher and B working as a singer in the local bar.

Given Circumstance

A and B are having dinner at their home and engaging in a confrontation regarding the suspected infidelity of B.

Future Circumstance, Fears, and Hopes

A may fear that B has cheated, and the relationship will end. A may hope that B has not cheated and that they can stay together. On the other hand, B may fear that A will discover the truth and the relationship will break down. B may hope that A believes them, leading to the situation being resolved and being in the clear. These assumptions align with the script and dialogue, but remember that interpretations may vary.

TASK

1. Choose one character from the scene provided or your own scene and apply the theory you have learnt to the script, making your own decisions and backstory.
2. Evaluate your choices. Do they create high stakes for your character? Can you make more interesting choices increase the stakes without overcomplicating the scene?
3. Write down why your character cares and what this situation means to them.

Now that we have completed our essential preparation, it's time to focus on the character's objective.

What Does the Character Want? Discovering a True Objective

The audience craves authenticity. They want to be moved, to have their hearts touched and their senses awakened. They long to immerse themselves in the characters' story and become captivated by the narrative. We owe it to our audience to remain engaged. A self-indulgent performance solely focused on showing emotions instead of pursuing an objective can result in a loss of energy, pace, and clarity. It contributes to a lack of active listening as the actor becomes absorbed in forcing emotions rather than genuinely listening to the other character or the scene's environment.

Listening is an actor's most vital responsibility. Our role is to truthfully and honestly tell the story, and we can only achieve this by being present and not forcing emotions. True listening allows us to react instinctively and impulsively to our scene partner. As actors, we need to understand that humans communicate as a response to their thoughts. Acting is not simply about memorising and delivering lines, but about communicating messages between two people that elicit natural responses. Our work must be instinctual, so we need a technique that promotes active listening. Objectives help us to understand our character's motivations whilst also encouraging active listening. We have to listen to see if what we are saying is affecting our partner in the desired way.

So, what could be a potential objective for Script 2? The objective is not set in stone and may vary based on each actor's interpretation of the scene. It might even change within the scene, but it's usually beneficial to find a consistent objective to avoid overcomplicating things. The objective must be something the character feels strongly about and, once again, it must be supported by the script. The objective is what propels the character in the given scene, centred around their wants and needs in that particular moment. We must be specific with our objectives to find the true impulses behind our character's actions and avoid choosing "base" objectives. A base objective is a term I use to describe the initial objective that might spring to mind but perhaps could be stronger. In Script 2, we could say that B wants to A to believe them. Whilst true, this base objective doesn't really encourage us to explore the layers within character B's dialogue. Whilst this more obvious objective choice might propel the actor into being convincing, perhaps a more interesting choice backed up by the script can be made. How would an objective of "I want you to recognise you're being crazy" change the performance? Perhaps now not only will the actor convince, but they may also manipulate, mock, ridicule, and blame. A base objective is always useful to start with but don't be afraid to challenge it and go further into the character's true underlying intentions.

In every interaction, we have base desire or need, and we have a deeper one. Right now, as the writer, my desire is for you, the reader, to continue reading and learning, whilst you may want me to teach you. My base objective is to write a book, but what I want from you is to stay engaged and to learn. When I shift my focus to what I want on a deeper level, my writing becomes clearer, more captivating, more entertaining, and insightful. If I solely focused on writing a book, the words might lack passion, drive, or care. When we create a deeper objective that centres around a desire or need from the person or object we are interacting with, something special happens – we become more active and interesting in the scene. So what do you want to do to the other person or thing in the scene? It could be to make them feel reassured, loved or scared. The key is to make the objective about them, not you. To achieve this, we use the formula "I want you to [action]". By creating an objective that focuses on the other person in the formula, we become actively engaged in our task as we aim to pursue something very real.

Consider these examples: I want you to tell the truth, I want you to back off, I want you to open up, I want you to apologise, I want you to laugh. The actor now has a tangible, measurable goal to authentically fight for. By actively listening to your co-actor, you can assess their reactions to see if you are acquiring your objective. Are your efforts making them laugh? Are you forcing them out of the room? Are you persuading them to tell the truth? The actor is now fighting for something very real, without pretence or fakery. In an exercise, I provided two students with a character brief and a script. The rest of the class was unaware of the storyline and hadn't seen the script. The script focused on an argument between characters A and B, primarily centred around lies about money issues and serious debt. After giving the students some time to familiarise themselves with the script, I asked them to deliver their interpretation of the story, focusing on a specific emotion assigned to each of them. Actor 1 was to embody anger, nothing else, and maintain it throughout. Actor 2 was assigned the emotion of sadness. The remaining students observed as the scene unfolded.

Actor 1 raised their voice, displayed exaggerated movements, and embodied the cliche behaviours associated with anger. They represented anger effectively and committed to the performance. Actor 2 also portrayed sadness well. They lowered their voice, kept their head down, and limited their movements. When I asked the observing students about their impressions of the scene, they commented on the actors' strong commitment to the emotions and how they could sense the emotions conveyed. They deemed it a good performance. However, when I asked them what the scene's storyline was, they struggled to answer. They didn't know, mentioning there was some sort of lie involved. There was a lack of clarity regarding the narrative itself. One student mentioned seeing an outburst of hate. When I inquired about the story's trajectory, the student couldn't recall what the story was about. Another student mentioned that whilst the actors were great at showing emotion, they grew bored as the scene didn't seem to escalate. Both actors appeared stuck in their emotions and not engaging with each other. Actor 1 couldn't escalate further because Actor 2 was too consumed by sadness and not listening to them. The scene had reached a standstill. The truth, storyline, and heart of the scene were lost.

Once the feedback was provided, I instructed the actors to repeat the exercise. This time, they were not to play angry or sad but instead had a specific objective they needed to fight for. I reiterated that it was important for them to listen to their co-actor to assess if their objective was being met and to allow their co-actor to impact them so that they could change their approach if it wasn't working. Actor 1's objective was "I want you to wake up and realise the effects of your actions", whilst Actor 2's objective was "I want you to help me". This shift in approach brought about a transformation in the actors' performances. By solely focusing on their motivations, they manipulated, patronised, belittled, guilted, attacked, and begged their partner. Ironically, through this process, genuine organic emotions of sadness, betrayal, guilt, and anger began to emerge in their performances. The two actors engaged with each other, creating a dynamic power struggle. When I asked for feedback from the observers this time, they remarked that the acting felt more authentic. The performance exhibited different dynamics, subtle nuances, and a heightened level of energy. The observers grasped that the story revolved around deceit and money, and they also understood each character's perspective and what they were fighting for. The audience expressed sympathy for the characters, sensing that real emotion was surfacing through the actors' portrayals.

I firmly believe that the use of objectives, particularly during the rehearsal process, is crucial for any actor. Merely faking emotions is no longer sufficient in today's era of high definition screens and cameras. When we strive for something genuine, we are never pretending. Instead of displaying emotions, we pursue an attainable goal and utilise our partner's reactions to inform our next response. This requires us to not only listen to the words spoken by our co-actor but to also pay attention to their tone, body language, and essence. Essentially, this technique allows us to replicate real life.

As mentioned earlier, every interaction has a purpose or need (objective). By identifying that need, we can understand our character's motivation and drive in the scene. When the other character in the scene still leaves us despite our efforts to keep them close, it will pull a real, authentic response from us – a true sense of loss, sadness, and frustration. This is not something we pretend, but rather something that is organically created. Whilst we must certainly be aware of the emotional context behind the scene, we should avoid relying solely on showcasing an emotion to inform our approach.

Now, let's consider potential objectives for Script 2:

A wants B to stay and talk.

B wants A to back off.

TASK

1. Determine a base objective for a character in Script 2 or your own script.

2. Transform the objective into an active one that revolves around the other person using the format: "I want you to [action]." For example, cry, back off, listen, awaken, shut up, sweat, calm down, love, fight.

Deepening the Choice

Is the objective as powerful as it could be? Let's consider the above objective: A wants B to stay and talk. Now, ask yourself the question: why? Well, because they want answers. So, A wants B to give them answers. Correct. This objective is already stronger, more precise, and carries an attitude. But why do they want answers? Because they need to know the truth. Why? Because they need to know if they have a future with B. So A wants B to confirm if they have a future together or not. This objective is stronger, more precise, but also encompasses a lot more vulnerability and stake from the character.

One time, I worked one-on-one with a student on a scene from *The Notebook*. The scene involves the two main characters, Allie and Noah, who were previously very much in love and have rekindled their relationship after years apart. After spending a few days together, Allie's mum shows up. Allie's mum had previously tried to convince her to stay away from Noah, who comes from a working-class background. Noah was never accepted by Allie's parents, and he believes their opinion hasn't changed, especially now that Allie is engaged to a very wealthy and respected man. This conversation between Allie and Noah takes place after Allie's mother discovers the affair. In the altercation, we learn that Allie's fiancé has also arrived. Noah and Allie engage in a dispute about how to move forward. To provide further context, here is the dialogue between the characters.

Script from 'The Notebook', Nicholas Sparks, (2004)

Noah: Interesting morning?

Allie: Yeah…Ben's here in town.

Noah: …He's here?

Allie: Yeah, we saw his car on the way…at the hotel.

Noah: Huh…I see you got my letters… (Allie nods) Finally.

Noah: …What are you gonna do, Al?

Allie: …I don't know…

Noah: We're back to that? Are we back there? What about the past couple of days? They happened you know.

Allie: I know that they happened, and they were wonderful. But they were also very irresponsible. (Noah gets up angrily, overturning a chair) Ben is waiting for me, and he's gonna be crushed when he finds out what I did!

Noah: So, you kiss me, and then you go back to your boyfriend? Was that your plan? Was that a test that I didn't pass?

Allie: No! I gave him my word.

Noah: And your word is shot to hell now, don't you think?

Allie: I don't know— I don't know. I'll find out when I talk to him.

Noah: This is not about keeping your promise, and it's not about following your heart. It's about security.

Allie: What is that supposed to mean?

Noah: Money!

Allie: What are you talki–

Noah: He's got a lot of money!

Allie: Now I hate you!

Noah: Well, I hate you. If you leave here, I hate you.

Allie: Wha– Haven't you been paying attention to anything that's been happening these past few days?

Noah: I guess not. I guess I must have misread all those signals.

Allie: Yeah, I guess you did.

Noah: You're bored! You're bored and you know it. You wouldn't be here if there wasn't something missing.

Allie: You arrogant piece of...

Noah: Would you just stay with me?

Allie: Stay with you? What for? Look at us, we're already fighting!

Noah: Well, that's what we do! We fight! You tell me when I'm being arrogant, and I tell you when you're being a pain in the ass! Which you are, 99% of the time. I'm not afraid to hurt your feelings. They have like a two-second rebound rate and then you're back doing the next pain-in-the-ass thing.

Allie: So what?

Noah: So it's not gonna be easy. It's gonna be really hard, and we're gonna have to work at this every day, but I wanna do that because I want you. I want all of you, forever.

Allie: No matter what I do, somebody gets hurt!

Noah: Would you stop thinking about what everyone wants? Stop thinking about what I want, what he wants, what your parents want. What do you want? (Allie shakes her head) What do you want?

Allie: It's not that simple–

Noah: What do you want? Goddammit, what do you want?!

Allie: ...I have to go.

In the session, my student, Ben, portrayed the character of Noah, whilst I played Allie. When I asked him what his objective was, Ben said, "I want Allie to stay with me." Ben's response wasn't wrong, as Noah makes this very clear in the script. However, I wanted him to dig deeper and uncover what truly drives Noah, allowing us to unearth vulnerability and depth.

"Why?" I asked.

"Because he loves her and he knows that they belong together," Ben replied.

"So, Noah wants Allie to realise they belong together?" I suggested.

"No, Noah wants Allie to admit they belong together," Ben clarified.

"Why?" I continued.

"Because she already knows they belong together, and it's other people that are confusing her. She came back to him after all these years, so that means something, right?" Ben explained.

"So, what does Noah really want from Allie? What does he repeatedly do or say in the script?" I asked.

"He challenges her to make her own decisions," Ben replied. After a few moments, Ben turned to me and said, "Noah wants Allie to follow her heart and make her own decisions for once."

A strong, well-understood, and carefully considered objective will change your entire performance. I always recommend that you go through the same thought process that Ben did to uncover your characters' true objectives.

Here are a set of rules to follow when choosing an objective:

1. Keep it simple. Your objective should be a relatively short sentence.

2. Make it strong and specific. Avoid weak objectives like, "I want you to know", or "I want you to care". Instead, opt for something that prompts action, such as "I want you to listen", or "I want you to fight for us".

3. Keep asking "why?" Challenge your objective to strengthen it.

4. Try the opposite of your chosen objective. If your objective is "I want you to love me", try "I want you to hate me". Exploring the opposite can reveal deeper inner conflicts.

5. You can utilise more than one objective in a scene, but exercise this with caution. In most cases, the objective doesn't need to change if you've found the right one. There may be instances where your character's viewpoint significantly shifts within a scene due to new information, in such cases, consider that the character may still desire the initial objectives deep down, but the events have introduced another desire. Try to maintain the same objective whilst acknowledging the presence of an additional objective that creates internal conflict. Avoid utilising more than two objectives in one scene unless absolutely necessary. You should also avoid overcomplicating things; simplicity is key. We want to minimise excessive thinking, as it hinders our ability to be present.

6. During the performance, be aware of your objective before running the scene, but trust that you have done the work. Make listening your priority. At this point, let go of the the-

ory and act with instinct, drive, and impulse. We will talk more about these skills later in this book.

TASK

1. Consider how you can deepen the choice on your character's objective for Script 2 or your own script.

Remember, the objective is a key phrase or reminder of your character's deep intention or goal, but it should not overshadow the importance of listening and responding during the performance. To truly connect to our scene partner, avoid solely focusing on the objective to the point where you stop receiving. Always remain open and receptive to your partner. By using an objective in a scene and genuinely listening to our partner, we assess whether we are achieving our objective or not. If we find ourselves falling short, we can adjust our approach and the actions we employ to attain what we want. This leads us to the next chapter, where we will consider *how* our characters achieve their objective. We do this by exploring actions.

9. Actions and the "How"

How do we achieve what we want in life? In every life scenario, we have an objective. As discussed earlier, our words and movements always serve a purpose, and there is always a desired outcome behind everything we do. That is our objective. When we order a coffee, it could be to quench a thirst or satisfy an addiction. When we smile at someone on the street, it might be to spread joy, diffuse hostility, or alleviate unease. The "how" of getting what we want is where the real fun lies in acting.

TASK

1. Reflect on your activities today and consider any objectives you had. Write them down. Then, think about how you achieved these objectives. For example, if you wanted your mum to buy you a pair of shoes, you may have resorted to methods like bribery, encouragement, begging, or manipulation.

In acting technique, it's best to think of "how" we get what we want as the "action". Nick Moseley states in the book *Actioning* (2016, Pg 7) that Actioning was developed in the 1970's by The Joint Stock Theatre Company but often people mistake the technique as a Stanislavski method. This technique of 'actioning' has been used throughout my career and is an acting technique taught at most drama schools and acting classes. It is a technique I have found particularly useful helping me to increase understanding of the characters intention within a script. Throughout this book, we will use the term "action" to refer to the "how". The action we choose is always centred around the other person; essentially, we are trying to influence them in some way to achieve our objective. Simply put, we must consider what we are doing to the other person, situation, or thing to attain what we want. To understand this process better, I recommend breaking each line into thoughts to identify our thought triggers.

A thought represents the central meaning behind what you are saying. When we communicate, we don't speak in sentences but in thoughts. A thought trigger is what prompts you to say what you say. Why is there a need to express it? It becomes glaringly obvious in a performance when an actor doesn't know the reason behind their lines beyond the fact it's written in the script. As actors, we must put in the work to understand the motivations behind each thought and every line. Usually, each thought will have a different motivation, and different motivations will typically require different actions. Breaking the script into thoughts makes it easier for us to connect our actions with the dialogue. It also helps actors identify shifts and changes in thoughts within the script, ultimately enhancing their delivery. Rest assured; this technique is not as complicated as it may sound.

A thought trigger is the stimulus that prompts your speech, movement, or reaction. It is your response to a given stimulus. Consider how we communicate in real life. We encounter a stimulus, which could be communication from another person or a visual from an external source, like seeing a blue butterfly. This stimulus serves as the thought trigger. The trigger then generates a thought, such as recalling a friend who passed away who loved butterflies. This thought leads to a reaction. It might manifest as tears, sharing stories about the friend, or even falling silent. Regardless of the specific reaction, it arose from a thought trigger.

When a trigger occurs, a thought emerges, inspiring us to convey a message to the person or thing we are communicating with. The message itself is what holds the upmost significance, not the specific words used to convey that message. The specific words used are based on the writer's vision of how that character speaks because of their social and historical background and so do hold much weight in terms of characterisation however in terms of understanding character motivations it is the message that is the important part. In our everyday communication, we don't consciously deliberate on the precise words or movements we will use; it happens almost subconsciously (based on our upbringing, education, and other factors such as the people we surround ourselves with and the audience we speak with). Instead, we focus on the message we want to convey and utilise words and movement to articulate our message to the recipient. Simply put, a stimulus affects our senses, serving as the thought trigger. This thought trigger then generates a thought, which influences the message we wish to communicate.

Stimulus → Thought Trigger → Message → Response/Communication

Within a script, some sentences convey a single main thought whilst others are divided into multiple thoughts. It's rare for the same thought to span across two sentences. Why repeat the message twice? Writers don't repeat words or sentences without purpose; it's usually to express a new emotion, irritation, impatience, and so on. Thoughts are also connected to "beats", which are non-spoken moments in the script. Remember, a thought is a message the character wishes to communicate, and when that message changes, it becomes a new thought. Let's break down the script into thoughts and assign numbers to label them accordingly.

Let's work through Script 2 as an example. We will break up Character B's thoughts.

A: Do you have anything to say?

B: 1. They were harmless messages.

A: They were explicit messages.

B: 2. Oh, give over, it was just a joke. (Some people may prefer to split this into two thoughts).

A: Are you sure?

B: 3. Of course I am sure, 4. What exactly are you accusing me of here?

A: I think you know what I'm saying.

B: 5. There was nothing in those messages. 6. It was harmless banter, 7. but maybe you wouldn't understand that because you're too busy snooping through my phone!

A: Yeah, with good right. Now you either tell me the truth or…

B: 8. Or what? 9. I am telling you the truth! 10. What do you want me to do? 11. Shall we call him? 12. Do you want me to call Dave?

A: No.

B: 13. Because you know you are being irrational.

A: No, because he would never own up to it, would he? I just need you to tell me. If you're playing me for a fool, I need you to tell me.

B: 14. You're being stupid.

A: Don't call me that.

B: 15. How could you think that I would do something like this to you? 16. I love you. 17. I would never hurt you.

BEAT.

B: 18. You need to think about what just happened here, because if you want this, there needs to be trust involved.

B: 19. GOES TO LEAVE.

A: Where are you going?

B: 20. I need to get out of here.

TASK

1. Find a script and break it down into thoughts by numbering each thought.

2. Consider the thought trigger. Why do you speak or say what you say? What prompted your reaction?

Note that people may break down the script in different ways, and interpretations of thoughts may vary. For instance, "Oh, give over, it was just a joke" could be seen as two separate thoughts by some, which would impact the delivery of the lines. The first thought, "Oh, give over", might imply "please stop talking", whilst the second thought, "it was just a joke", could convey "you're overreacting". In this case, I've chosen to keep it as one continuous thought because the overarching message is to defuse the situation. Once the script is broken down into thoughts, it's time to assign actions. Remember, an action represents "how" we achieve our objective.

For example:

Objective: I want you to like me.

Action: I amuse you.

Each thought in the script will have its own action attached to it. We often express this as "I _ you", with a transitive verb in the blank space. A transitive verb is a verb that prompts action from a person or thing. For example, if my objective is "I want you to leave", I could try various approaches to achieve this. I could condescend to you, bully you, patronise you, bribe you, scare you, warn you, or embarrass you. If these actions don't work, I can change my tactics and try something else.

Now let's look at Character B. In this conversation, Character A serves as the main stimulus for Character B, and what Character A says or does becomes Character B's thought trigger – the thing that prompts a thought. Character B's thought then leads to a message that they want to communicate.

A **(Stimulus to B)**: "Do you have anything else to say?" **(Character B's thought trigger)**.

B **(Stimulus to A)**: "They were harmless messages." **(Character B's message in response to the thought trigger)**.

Remember:

1. The stimulus is the person or thing you interact with (see/taste/touch/smell).
2. The thought trigger is what prompts you to think a thought.

3. The thought produces a response in the form of a message you wish to communicate. This interaction pattern applies to all interactions in life.

The way actors pursue their objectives may vary depending on the individual. That's the beauty of acting – no two performances are ever exactly the same. One actor may interpret the thought trigger with hostility, resulting in a defensive reply, whilst another actor may perceive it with fear, leading to a more vulnerable and desperate response. The key is to align our actions with our own interpretation of the thought trigger. You may find it helpful to write down your attitude towards the thought trigger on the script. Does it make your character feel irritated or attacked? If so, your character might respond by mocking or belittling Character A. This becomes your action. There's no right or wrong answer here as long as your choice aligns with the narrative and the author's intention. Essentially, all you need to remember is that an action represents the "how" of achieving what we want, and it is always focused on the other person. Whilst the format "I _ you" is useful to do this, don't feel limited to this format. Some people, including myself, struggle to adhere to it and may take time to find the right word, especially in time-sensitive moments. In my opinion, the format is not crucial; what matters is understanding how you want to affect your scene partner. For example, "I make you feel stupid" works just as effectively as "I belittle you". If you're having trouble finding a transitive verb, write it down in a way that works for you, but always ensure it reflects how you want to affect the other person. *Actions* by Marina Caldarone and Maggie Lloyd-Williams is a helpful transitive verb thesaurus that I highly recommend you consider purchasing. It's one of the books I consider to be essential for any actor and has been a valuable tool throughout my career.

If you want to explore actions in more depth, spend a few hours with a child. Children are exceptional at playing this game; they master the art of using actions to get what they want. When denied chocolate, a child will employ various actions to persuade you to change your mind. They may misbehave to upset you, cry to evoke guilt, or annoy you by asking repeatedly, but they won't give up. Children are persistent and skilled at adapting their actions to get what they want. In our scenes, we must tap into our inner child to stay playful and open to variation. Remember, regardless of the action chosen, it must always align with our objective.

As humans, we possess an in-built system that allows us to engage in different tactical games and assess their effectiveness. When they don't work, we adjust our approach. This process is usually unconscious, but it can also be a conscious choice. One of my students asked me, "So it's a form of manipulation?" I replied, "I suppose, in a way, yes." However, manipulation carries negative connotations, and not every objective arises from a negative place. I view it more as a survival programme we have developed. It's a modern-day survival instinct embedded in our language. Whilst explaining this technique to a student, they questioned why they couldn't just play angry or upset, focusing solely on the emotion. Of course, we need to understand our character's emotional state within the scene; however, if all we do is play the state or emotion, our focus becomes fragmented, and the story and character journey within the scene become lost. When we use an action, our focus shifts to the other person and the impact we have on them, as well as the impact they have on us. We are pursuing something real, just as we do in life. During a heated discussion between two people, their focus is not solely on the anger; the anger is a consequence of the argument. Their focus is to convey their point, to make the other person listen or back down so that they feel heard. If our focus is only on the emotion, we may lose the driving force in the scene. The scene runs the risk of losing pace, energy, and movement, ultimately leading to viewer boredom. Whilst viewers appreciate emotional expression, if that is all they see, they start to disengage. It's like encountering someone who always puts on a show of tears;

eventually, it loses its impact. Our emotions should be affected as a result of the action in the scene and the relationship we have with our scene partner through listening and engaging rather than through forced displays.

I encourage my students to experiment with multiple actions in the rehearsal room. This allows actors to explore more interesting and unconventional choices and discourages pre-planned performances. In the actual performance, actions are set aside, and we focus solely on listening and responding to our co-actor. Actioning a script prompts us to consider the attitude and meaning behind our character's lines. Actions also help actors avoid self-indulgent performances by focusing on a tangible goal and something genuinely achievable, rather than simply playing a state. If I ask a student to portray sadness, they will "act" sad. However, if I instruct them to guilt their scene partner, they become active and start doing something that genuinely affects their partner. This often leads to a natural change in their own emotional state. Remember, an action is always something we do to the other person and usually follows the "I [transitive verb] you" model. This places the emphasis on the other person and shifts the focus away from us.

As mentioned earlier, we apply actions to different thoughts, not sentences. Each new thought carries a new intention, so it requires a new action. Let's take the previous script and quickly assign actions to it. Before we do that, let's create our objectives:

Objectives.

A wants B to confirm if they have a future together or not.
B wants to convince A that it is all in their head.

Remember: Actions must align with your objectives.

A: Do you have anything to say? (I question you)

B: They were harmless messages. (I answer you)

A: They were explicit messages. (I confront you)

B: Oh, give over, it was just a joke. (I dismiss you)

A: Are you sure? (I question you)

B: Of course I am sure (I convince you). What exactly are you accusing me of here? (I accuse you)

A: I think you know what I'm saying. (I counter you)

B: There was nothing in those messages. (I reject you) It was harmless banter, but maybe you wouldn't understand that because you're too busy snooping through my phone! (I accuse you)

A: Yeah, with good right! (I defy you) Now you either tell me the truth or… (I warn you)

B: Or what? (I "out" you) I am telling you the truth! (I awaken you) What do you want me to do? (I question you). Shall we call him? (I ask you) Do you want me to call Dave? (I interrogate you)

A: No. (I dismiss you)

Okay, so we have actioned the script, but have we done it with deep analysis or just surface-level analysis? Some of the actions applied such as "question" and "answer" are accurate but seem a bit unimaginative. Yes, we are asking and answering our scene partner things, but *how* do we do it? What is the subtext or possible attitude? Are we asking in a derogatory way to belittle or are we interrogating to assert our own authority? The problem with these actions is that they fall into what I call "practical actions" – they state things as they are with not an awful lot of interpretation around them. Examples of practical actions include question, ask, answer, offer, tell, teach, and inform. Whilst using practical actions provides clarity, they are rather boring and lack imagination and if you see them in your script, it would be a good idea to challenge them. It's worth noting the practical action on the page but try to explore more imaginative alternatives. Instead of "I ask you", try "I challenge you" or "I grill you". Suddenly, we have a strong attitude attached, one that creates a deeper emotional connection. Practical actions offer limited playfulness in performance and may result in a bland performance. Be courageous when selecting your actions, ensuring they align with your interpretation of the character. Ask yourself why your character behaves or reacts in a certain way. What are they trying to achieve? Don't take the easy route – think outside the box and make bold choices. This is what will make your performance unique and unlike anyone else's.

We want actions that inspire vulnerability and range. Vulnerability is essential for the audience to relate to a character, and range prevents the audience from growing tired of the performance. Both elements are necessary for a performance to be truthful and memorable. Now, let's go through the script again and carefully consider the actions and thoughts on a deeper level, avoiding practical actions and excessive repetition. We should think less practically and more deeply about how our character's attitude influences their behaviour.

Objectives.

A wants B to confirm if they have a future together or not.

B wants to convince A that it is all in their head.

Remember: actions must align with your objective.

So, let's break down the scene again with stronger, more goal-oriented actions. I'll explain the rationale behind the new actions.

A: Do you have anything to say? (I pressure you).

We're questioning them, but there's more to it than that. We could choose a softer approach, such as "I encourage you", to allow for vulnerability. However, as this is the first line in a dispute, I believe a high-energy, high-stakes action feels more appropriate. Remember, a "stake" is a term that refers to what our character "has to lose". In this scenario the stake is the relationship.

B: They were harmless messages. (I belittle you)

B is trying to defuse the situation and counter the attack. One way to do this is by making the other person feel small.

A: They were explicit messages. (I condescend you)

A needs to reinforce their point, status, opinion, and power. They assert control and ownership of their claim.

B: Oh give over, it was just a joke. (I mock you)

Here, a new action is played to make A feel stupid, with the intention of getting them to back down. Always link the action to the objective.

A: Are you sure? (I challenge you)

Another option would be a softer approach, such as "I beg you", which would show more desperation and vulnerability. But I've chosen a tougher interpretation, as I believe A would stick by their guns and confront B at this point.

B: Of course I am sure (I reassure you).

Deflection, belittling, and insulting actions haven't worked, so a new action is needed. This softer approach allows for variation and encourages vulnerability as the character becomes less aggressive.

What exactly are you accusing me of here? (I guilt you)

Guilt encourages A to reflect on their own actions and accusations and their part in this.

A: I think you know what I'm saying. (I defy you)

A is resisting B's attempts to regain power; they believe they are in the right.

B: There was nothing in those messages. (I block you)

Annoyed at A's defiance, B switches gears; their previous, methods of convincing haven't worked, and this leads to possible frustration. They back off from A with a plan to shut them down for good.

It was harmless banter, but maybe you wouldn't understand that because you're too busy snooping through my phone! (I expose you)

A repetition of an earlier point suggests rising tensions, increased irritation, and volatility. An attack on A comes into play. My interpretation of the character leads me to the action "expose", as they highlight the lack of trust that A has shown by going through their phone and it is a clear tactic to manipulate the situation.

A: Yeah, with good right! (I insult you).

A counters with an insult, standing by their accusations and not giving in to the guilt or insults thrown their way they.

Now you either tell me the truth or… (I threaten you)

Feeling a loss of control, A issues an ultimatum, attempting to make B fearful of losing them.

B: Or what? (I provoke you) I am telling you the truth! (I unsettle you) What do you want me to do? (I challenge you) Shall we call him? (I warn you) Do you want me to call Dave? (I scare you)

At this point, the ultimatum has had a negative impact on B, and they begin to feel the pressure. A range of actions could be used here to manipulate A into a submission.

A: No. (I stop you)

Cornered, A doesn't want a bruised ego. Understanding that the call could be potentially embarrassing and unproductive, they are the ones now backed in a corner.

You only need to action your own character in the script. Remember that actions provide possible ways to deliver the lines, but they are never planned or set in stone as we must respond to what our co-actor is sending us. An actor's fundamental job in the actual performance is to receive, listen, and respond. At this point, I would also suggest experimenting with opposite actions in your rehearsals. For example, in an argument, what happens if you try to make the other person laugh instead of cry? Consider this: how many times, when you have been angry or upset, have you tried to "amuse someone" to deflect from the difficult situation? It is worth considering the opposite action and trying it out.

There are some key principles to follow when actioning. Always remember that actions should:

1. Appear on every thought.
2. Run linear with your character's overarching objective.
3. Have an attitude attached to them.
4. Be exciting, avoiding practical offers.
5. Be varied, avoiding repetition.
6. Changed, played with, and never cemented in the actual performance.

TASK

1. Action your script.
2. Write down two additional actions for each thought, including the opposite action.

10. Actioning in Practice

Now that we have written out our actions, it's time to test them. Work through each thought and apply the corresponding action, either with your scene partner during rehearsals or on your own. If you're working alone, I recommend filming yourself if possible so you can assess your level of commitment to each action. When applying the actions to the lines, observe the impact by watching the other person (or yourself on playback) to determine whether they are effective and feel right. If the actions are not working or the performance seems monotone, I encourage you to first challenge yourself and see if you are truly committing to the action. It's possible that the action might make you uncomfortable or that you hold a judgement towards it, which can affect your level of commitment. I challenge you to push through the discomfort and fully commit to the action. Immerse yourself in the story, activate your imagination, and remember your job as an actor. If you feel you're committing but the action still isn't working, then it may be time to explore a new action.

Sometimes the actions we have chosen don't feel right or they don't have the desired effect on the other person. It could be that the action is too much of a jump from the previous action or that it doesn't quite work with what our partner is feeding us. We've all seen actors go from zero to a hundred in a very short period of time; one minute they're calm, and the next they're screaming. This can be very jarring for the audience because it's not how humans typically behave. The director may also have a different interpretation of your character's behaviours in the scene, which might require a change in your approach. Regardless, if an action isn't working or resonating, the solution is always the same: change it and try something new.

Actions are not set in stone; they can be flexible. I encourage you to play with them during rehearsals if something isn't working, don't be afraid to let it go and try something new. We want performances that are not constrained by limitations, but rather thrive. Remember, we're trying to replicate real life, and in real life, we employ a variety of actions to fulfil a need. When we argue with our spouse and we want to get them to agree with us (objective), we might insult, flatter, persuade, shock, stun, melt, beg, or awaken them. It's through this exploration of actions that we become more flexible on set.

Experimenting with actions enables us to understand our character's intentions and internal conflicts more deeply, approaching and exploring the character with multiple possibilities. When exploring these possibilities, make sure you wholeheartedly commit to the action. If your action is to "fight", can you fight harder? If your action is to "guilt", can you intensify it? How are you using space between the lines and pauses to further explore this action? Be competitive with your use of actions and fight for your status/power or voice in the scene. In life, humans constantly engage in status battles, and acting is no different. Every interaction is a game of status, whether we're shifting it as friends or fighting for higher status as foes. During the process of playing status shifts with your scene partner, remember to have fun. Explore the various ways you can impact your scene partner and affect them; that's what acting is all about. Listen to what they offer and respond in light of that with an action that aligns with your objective. Whilst it's important to make an impact, never forget to receive and listen. Sometimes actors become so engrossed in their own actions that they stop listening to their partner and allowing their partner to affect them. During the rehearsal process, consciously observe whether you're truly open to being affected by the other person. Once you feel that your actions have been thoroughly explored and practised, and you have a deep understanding of your character's motivations for each line, it's time to forget about them.

Actions should be used thoughtfully and with intention during the rehearsal process. Exploring a variety of actions allows for flexibility in your reading and a deeper understanding of the script. However, it's important to note that actioning should never be used to rigidly plan or secure a performance. As actors, our primary task is to listen and respond truthfully, and a planned performance works in conflict with this idea. The actioning process allows us to understand our character's motivations and how we can affect the other person to achieve our objectives, but when performing on screen, we should let go of conscious thoughts about our actions. Once you feel you have fully grasped your character's motives, it's time to release all the groundwork and trust your instincts. In the final stages of the performance process, focus on being fully present and truly listening to your scene partner. Allow yourself to be affected by them and immerse your imagination in the scene as much as possible. To do this effectively, free your mind from excessive technique. Embrace spontaneity and let life flow into your performance. Don't think too much about actions; instead, react truthfully and be completely present. Be aware of your character's desires and needs but engage fully with the action unfolding before you. The work you've done so far has helped you understand your character on a deeper level, enabling you to react instinctively and almost subconsciously. Now it's time to let go.

TASK

1. Play, experiment and explore your actions.

2. Work with a scene partner or film yourself delivering the lines to the camera. Can you push your actions further? Are you playing it too safe? Are you committing? Identify any barriers to committing and address them.

3. If any actions don't work, change them and find a better fit.

4. Play, play, and play some more. Once you feel a thorough understanding of your character's motivations and intentions, try the opposite actions as well.

5. Let go of all preconceived notions. Listen, react, be fully present, and enjoy the performance.

11. Learning Your Script

If you have been working with the tasks provided, you may have already learnt most, if not all, of the script. However, if you still need to memorise or perfect the lines, there are a couple of techniques you can use.

As actors, we should know our lines so well that they flow instinctively from our tongues. The lines should be embedded in our subconscious, firmly imprinted in our mind, so that we don't have to think about them during a performance. The first method is repetition – run through the lines over and over again. Read the script first thing in the morning, throughout the day, and last thing before bed. We are in an alpha brain wave state just before we go to sleep and right after we wake up which means we are more receptive to absorbing information. It's the perfect time to start the memorisation process. I recommend starting this routine as soon as you receive the script. At this point, focus on reading the lines aloud without placing too much emphasis on intonation or specific delivery. Let your mouth remember the movement without rigidly memorising the exact way to say the lines as we want flexibility here.

I also suggest reading and reciting the lines whenever you get a chance throughout the day. I've had countless moments where people gave me weird looks whilst I recited lines on the train or in a coffee shop. The goal is to know them so well they become ingrained in your subconscious. If you can recite them whilst doing other things like chores or shopping, then they have truly become ingrained into your subconscious. Eventually, through muscle memory and repetition, the lines will flow effortlessly from your tongue, in the same way your phone number or address does. Some actors find it useful to record the lines and listen to them on repeat. This is a useful tool when you're out and about, as you can play the lines whilst working out at the gym or shopping. There are many line-learning apps available that you can explore to find the one that suits you.

Sometimes, certain lines or parts of the script may be harder to learn. It could be because you don't fully understand your character's responses or motivations. If that's the case, you need to put in more work on these problem areas of the script. Highlight the problematic sections and examine the thought trigger that precedes your line (usually the dialogue or action). Try to understand why your character would respond the way they do based on that thought trigger.

Ask yourself these key questions:

1. What action occurred before your line?
2. How did you feel about it?
3. How did that inform your reply?

Remember, we always work in thoughts, not lines. If you've connected the thoughts and understand the "why" behind your response, you only need to listen to your scene partner and you will remember your response (the thought). Working with thoughts instead of focusing solely on lines not only helps actors learn their lines easier and listen effectively, but it allows them to fully understand the emotional journey of the character they're portraying. I've seen so many actors in the past who only memorised lines by recalling them in sentence form. Even if they deliver the lines convincingly, the flow of the scene often feels off because they're not truly reacting to their scene partner but rather trying to remember their response. Some actors may insert awkward pauses in places that don't make sense, whilst others may use intonations that don't quite feel right. These errors often lead to unnatural performances because the focus becomes more about line memorisation than genuine listening, hindering the effective communication of the character's thoughts, needs, and desires. If you have done the work and the thought is there but the specific words are still not coming to you because this character talks in a certain way or uses certain words different to yourself, you have three options.

1. Perseverance through repetition. Record your cues on a voice note, leaving gaps for your responses. Repeat this process.
2. Research any unfamiliar words in the script and practice incorporating them into your everyday life.
3. Collaborate with the director to explore slight alterations to lines that won't drastically change their meaning. Like any skill, line memorisation improves with practice, so practice weekly.

TASK

1. Challenge yourself to learn a new script every week. Line learning, like any skill, can be strengthened with consistent effort.

12. Finding the Emotion

Generating organic emotion is often considered one of the hardest parts of the acting process. Actors put so much pressure on being able to cry on cue and emote. However, emotions come easier when they arise naturally and effortlessly through presence and relaxation and not force. Authentic emotion emerges when we are truly present and have a deep understanding of our character's desires and conflicts.

Whilst finding the emotion within the script is essential, solely focusing on this aspect can overshadow a well-balanced performance. Many actors fall into the trap of centring their performance around the question, "What emotion can I display here?" This narrow focus on emotion can result in a lack of character development and journey. It's safe to say that most actors have been guilty of this at some point. We all want to showcase a compelling performance, and emotionally driven portrayals are often the most memorable. However, it's important to avoid solely relying on emotions.

So how do we explore emotion in a scene? The key is to ask ourselves, "What are the main emotions present for each character?" Let's revisit Scene 2 to apply this theory. The answers to this question will vary according to each individual's interpretation of the script. One potential scenario is that A's baseline emotion is fear due to B's potential betrayal, whilst B's baseline emotion could be anger. Your choices may be different. Once we have identified the baseline emotions, we need to reconnect with them emotionally. When have we experienced similar emotions? How did they arise? What happens in the scene to evoke such emotions from the characters? What struggles and fights do they face? Can we relate to any of these experiences?

Finding the emotion is always about establishing a connection and developing empathy. Empathy is a crucial skill for actors. We must empathise with our characters to gain a greater understanding of their experiences and feel their struggles within our bodies, not just within our minds. If empathy isn't your strongest skill, you must take steps to strengthen it. Exercise your ability to empathise. Put yourself in the shoes of others, even those you may dislike. Practice being compassionate and try to understand other people's motivations and behaviours. How would you feel if you were in their position? What would their life feel like? By cultivating compassion and embracing different perspectives, you not only enhance your acting abilities but also nurture your own emotional intelligence.

TASK

1. Select a baseline emotion and note it on your script.

2. Reflect on the events that led the character to feel this way. Identify their struggles, fights, and the obstacles hindering their success or happiness.

3. Consider what this emotion means to you. Recall your own experiences or similar situations and immerse yourself in those memories. Connect with the feelings they evoke.

4. Practice empathy daily. When someone is rude to you, try to understand what might have triggered that response. Put yourself in the shoes of others regularly and imagine what life is like for them.

After researching your baseline emotion, perform the scene and observe your findings. Remember to listen and respond to your partner. If you're working alone, read the scene, including the other person's lines and ask yourself whether there are other emotions or even opposing emotions present in the scene. If Character A's baseline emotion is fear, are there moments when they feel safe? The same goes for Character B; if their baseline emotion is anger, are there any moments of peace or love?

Humans rarely feel just one emotion – hate and love often coexist. The internal conflicts we as humans feel is often the cause of raw organic emotion. I had an audition recently for the role of a woman reading a letter from her late dad on her wedding day to her wedding guests. During the speech I was overwhelmed with feelings of love but also loss and pain. This strong conflict of emotion that I felt became so heavy I started to cry. It is the internal conflict of love and loss and of love and pain that caused my tears. Focusing on only one side of the coin is sometimes not enough. Exploring multiple emotions also adds variety to your performance, creates light and shade, and allows for subtext and vulnerability. Think of a scene as a colour palette, where the colours (emotions) blend seamlessly. Your job as an actor is to discover the varying emotions in the scene that may be present and consider how they would impact your performance. Avoid attaching yourself to these emotions or planning specific responses based on them. Remember, this is an exploration, not a strategy or a fixed plan.

TASK

1. Identify other emotions present in the scene. Does the opposite emotion come into play at any point?
2. Read or perform the scene using this opposite emotion. Did you unearth anything significant?

Next, closely analyse your thought triggers and the emotional responses they may elicit in the script. Activate your imagination to really step into the characters' shoes. Take the time to focus on what your scene partner actually says and how it might emotionally impact your character. For example, if your partner tells you they no longer love you, how would your character feel? Has this ever happened to you? If not, can you activate your imagination to deeply resonate with this situation? Take note of words or scenarios that trigger specific emotional responses from you. As actors, our unique experiences are powerful tools that make our performances unlike anyone else's. To truly connect with what your character is going through, you must connect with yourself on a deep level.

It is important to consider the emotional journey depicted in the script. Where does your character begin emotionally, and how do things unfold for them? Let's look at Character A's possible emotional journey in Script 2. They might start off angry, launching an attack on their partner with fire in their belly, but as the scene progresses, they lose control, and fear creeps in, especially when B leaves the room. At that point, they may feel completely vulnerable, abandoned, and stupid. Understanding the character's journey is always recommended because every character should always experience some sort of change within a scene; otherwise, what would be the point? It also becomes extremely tedious to watch a character remain stuck in a single emotion throughout a scene.

Keep in mind that your scene partner's delivery of lines will impact your entire performance, so remain flexible. Avoid firm decisions on reactions and delivery; instead, give yourself options. During our actor preparation, we utilise potentials, not fixed decisions, as your performance is also dependent on your partner's performance and the director's vision. Perhaps your scene partner responds with love and kindness, evoking feelings of guilt and remorse, or maybe they attack you in a fit of rage, leaving you scared and desperate. Whatever the case may be, remember that staying true to the moment is paramount.

Allowing your partner to emotionally affect you can be the biggest hurdle you have to jump over as an actor, but like everything else, practice makes perfect. In performance, an actor's focus should always be on staying present, receptive, and responsive. Many actors mistakenly prioritise remembering lines, worrying about others' opinions, and self-judgement. If you find yourself caught in these concerns, ground yourself and stay present. Slow the scene down, truly listen, and fully engage. Once you feel that you have truly heard your partner and have allowed them to affect you, you can gradually increase the pace again. To quieten the voice of our own internal judge it is imperative that we live in the present and switch our focus away from ourselves and line reciting and onto our scene partner. This means that we have to trust ourselves and accept that what happens in that moment happens. There is no plan and there is no expectation from the scene. This can feel somewhat uncomfortable to an actor, but lean into it. To genuinely access our emotions, we must learn to self-trust and this might take some time. If you struggle with self-trust in your personal life this is likely to arise within your acting technique, so I would advise that you seek a skilled mindset coach to help you build your self-trust.

TASK

1. Examine the thought triggers and identify the emotions that may arise from them. Make a note of these emotions.
2. Consider the character's possible emotional journey. How might the character begin, and how could this evolve?
3. Run the scene again with this new understanding in mind.
4. Slow down the pace of the scene to truly listen and engage with your partner. Be flexible, open, and receptive to vulnerability.

The tasks are designed to encourage a deeper connection with your character's emotions. However, please do not focus solely on the emotions within the scene. If you do, the story is likely to be lost, and the viewer will only witness a display of emotion without gravitas, meaning, or a fulfilling journey. As actors, we must relate to and empathise with our characters, but we must also pay attention to their motivations, what they are fighting for, and what they may lose. When we direct our energy toward these aspects, genuine organic emotion can be discovered.

Forcing emotion in a scene compromises the character's fight and runs the risk of rendering the actor inactive. When absorbed only in emotion, the energy wanes, the performance becomes limited within a specific emotional range, and the scene lacks an engaging journey. The result? A disengaged audience. In every scene, your character is fighting for something, even in the darkest moments. Take, for example, a scene involving a character contemplating suicide. What is their fight? They are fighting for relief, for peace, because the world they are in right now is so agonising that they yearn to escape it. A fight encourages external drive, internal conflict, pace, and energy, and it is the combination of these elements that often generates authentic, organic emotion. Focusing solely on playing sadness, for instance, would only capture a fraction of the character's story. The other part, which reveals their desperation to find peace and the internal conflict of leaving loved ones behind, would be lost.

Actors must consider not only their character's emotions, but also their character's fights, deepest desires, drives, and fears. They must empathise with their character's journey, understand their character's pain, and really resonate with what their character stands to lose. Surface-layer emotional connection will only take you so far. An actor's job is not to present an emotion but to embody it.

When actors start playing a state, they may emphasise specific words or attempt to force the words to elicit an emotional response. They may use their body and voice in a stereotypical way associated with that emotion and remain locked in that state. For example, let's consider the emotion sadness. When an actor plays a state of sadness, they channel all their energy into trying to manufacture tears or force a display of emotion, rather than truly engaging with their scene partner and living the truth of the scene. They might rely on emotional memory, which ultimately confines them to their own past experiences, or they may dissociate from the scene as they exert all their energy in their body to produce an emotion. Essentially, the actor tries so hard to create an emotion that it compromises genuine, truthful emotion and actor presence.

Additional issues arise when actors claim to have felt something, assuming that it must look "right". That feeling is typically a memory of an emotion they once experienced, one that may not align with the current script but with their own personal history. Emotion memory and other techniques can certainly aid us in accessing emotions for a role, but it is often more effective to employ these techniques during scene preparation rather than during the actual performance. Forcing an emotion or re-living a past emotion can disrupt the flow of the performance. In real life, we never consciously think, "I am unhappy, so I will show it and act sad". Sadness is an emotional response and a reaction to a thought; it is the end result. So, how do we access this part of ourselves? The key aspects to focus on when finding the emotion in a scene are Preparation, Understanding, Empathy, Relatability, Stake, Imagination, Presence, Openness, Instinct, and Vulnerability. All of these topics will be discussed more extensively in later chapters of this book. However, for now, let me explain why each skill is essential for actors when accessing their emotions for a role.

Preparation: Some actors can easily access their emotions whilst others may need to develop a strategy. If you've been directed to cry, for example, then you may need to ensure that you are in a lower emotional state beforehand. A tool that has been useful for me is to prime myself into a lower mood ten to fifteen minutes before I step on set. I am not an actor who can go from laughing in the green room to crying within minutes. Preparation is therefore an essential and fundamental part of my acting process if I am to achieve the desired emotional state for a particular scene. Emotion memory, imagery, and music work wonders in changing my state into one suited for the character in the scene. Once my state has been changed and my mood lowered, I can access my emotions much more readily. Consider this, when you're on the edge of crying, even the slightest trigger can set you off. The same applies to anger. If you've experienced several frustrating incidents throughout the day, the smallest thing can push you over the edge.

Changing your physiology can help shift your emotional state. For a scene requiring excitement and happiness, you might jump up and down and laugh before entering the scene. If the scene calls for fear or apprehension, finding a way to speed up your breathing (such as running on the spot) can be effective. Additionally, tools that engage the senses and the mind, such as memories, music, or imagery, can be employed to alter your state. It's important to discover what works best for you as an actor. Many actors, me included, use triggers like images, memories, movements, or songs to evoke specific emotions. These triggers are best utilised before the scene. Avoid taking these into the scene as you may lose connection and presence.

Understanding: Do you fully understand what your character is going through and their objective? Do you feel confident with your understanding of the script and the character journey? Have you prepared thoroughly, honouring the author's intentions? Understanding your character's current motivations, fears, and desires is essential for comprehending their emotional turmoil. Understanding breeds confidence and confidence enhances commitment and freedom. Doubt, on the other hand, is the enemy of execution.

Empathy: Can you connect with your character on an emotional level? Can you cultivate a deep sense of compassion for your character? Can you place yourself in their shoes and truly feel what they are going through? Can you understand their pain, hardship, and struggles? Can you empathise even when portraying a villain or someone who has made morally questionable choices? Can you find a reason behind your character's behaviour? No one believes they are truly a bad person; they believe they are working toward something good or away from something painful. It is our job to find that perspective.

Relatability: Can you relate to the character to support your understanding of what this character is going through? Exploring the similarities between yourself and the character will help you on this quest. Perhaps you share a similar background, values, intellect, or physicality. Techniques such as Stanislavski's emotion memory and Uta Hagan's substitution can be useful tools here.

Emotion memory involves tapping into past memories that evoke similar emotions to what a character is experiencing in a given scene. Similarly, substitution is a technique where actors aim to connect with a character's situation by recalling a time that they went through something similar. For instance, if the character is going on a first date with a friend, which makes them feel excited but awkward, the actor may recall a time when they experienced a similar mix of excitement but awkwardness in a relationship. Alternatively, they could reflect on a situation where their expectations didn't align with reality.

Stake: Do you understand what your character has to win or to lose in their situation? Understanding the stakes will change the pace, energy, urgency, and fight in any given scene. Where are the stakes higher and where are they lower? Stakes allow the actor to understand their character's deepest fears and insecurities in a given moment, consequently adding to the conflict and tension within a scene. High stakes require much more actor commitment in the scene as the character has more to lose. Do you know what your character is fighting for? How are they fighting? Do they feel defeated or deflated, or are they strong, committed, and ready to take action? What obstacles do they need to overcome to achieve their goals? What are the consequences if they win the fight? What happens if they lose?

Imagination: An actor's imagination is one of their greatest tools as it allows them to immerse themselves fully in their character. To truly connect with our character's emotions, we must aim to understand them as best we can; surface-layer interpretations will not impact our audience. If we can activate our imagination, we can tap into a wider range of emotions and experiences which can aid a stronger emotional connection. This connection can allow the actor to produce naturally authentic emotions that will resonate with their audience. So, close your eyes, engage your imagination, and fully immerse yourself in your character's journey, battles, and struggles scene by scene. Take your time and allow for creativity and curiosity and dive into it, experiencing it in all of its depth. A strong active imagination will help the actor produce performances that are emotionally impactful and nuanced.

Presence: A present actor is an active actor. One that is focused and aware of their surroundings and reactive to the action around them. To be present, we must actively listen to our scene partner and our environment and allow it to affect us. We must be engaged and energised. Awake and free. Whilst the preparatory work is crucial, once we are on set, we must trust the process and prioritise listening, disregarding anything else that could be a distraction. This is the only way to achieve freedom, integrity, and authenticity in any given scene. When we are truly present, we can allow our scene partner to impact us emotionally. We can let their words resonate within us, helping us to execute a truthful performance with emotional expression.

Openness: Can you refrain from critical judgement, both of yourself and your scene partner? Can you ignore the internal judge in your head cursing your performance and your talent? Are you able to set aside preconceived notions and welcome any acting offers that arise during the scene? This could be a physical gesture like a hug, a raised voice, or the use of a prop. Can you collaborate with your scene partner and embrace new ideas and spontaneity? Can you remain open to receive whatever your partner throws your way without fear of it "going wrong"? Being open is about leaning into the unknown. When we are open to anything and refrain from judgement nothing is forced, ridiculed, or blamed and emotions arise naturally.

Instinct: Do you work with your instincts or against them? Society has taught us to suppress our emotions and our instincts. The consequences? Often we ignore them or even worse – we don't hear them. From a young age, we're told to grow up, hide our emotions, and be strong. This makes it challenging for actors to truly connect with their instincts as we have spent years trying to silence them. If an actor judges themselves when they display their emotions in public, if they see crying as weak or anger as shameful, they will be less likely to act on these emotions as their instinct will be to suppress them. Can you re-awaken your instincts? Can you create a stronger relationship with yourself and your emotions with no judgement attached?

Vulnerability: When an actor is vulnerable, they open themselves up to a variety of emotions and outcomes, which allows them to connect to their characters on a more profound level. Do you give yourself permission to be vulnerable? Are you in touch with your emotions? Can you open yourself to your scene partner, receiving and allowing their offerings? Can you expose parts of yourself that you often try to hide – your emotions, fears, and insecurities? Vulnerability means showing everything, the good the bad and the ugly. The transparency found in being vulnerable, I believe, is the gateway to emotional expression.

If you take the time to master these elements, you will master your emotional connection. It may mean that work on your own belief systems, self-trust, and self-acceptance is required. The second half of this book will help you with that. The following chapters will delve deeper into some of these topics.

13. Listening, Intuition, and Instinct

As actors, we fully embody our characters, immersing ourselves in every aspect of their lives, their history, and their journey as truthfully as possible. We strive to make the audience believe, relate, and feel, inspiring them to continue watching. Creating this imaginary world is a collaborative effort. Our connection with the audience is crucial – if we fail to engage them, they won't care. To convincingly portray the intricate interactions of real life, we much simulate real life itself. In our daily lives, we are all listeners, albeit to varying degrees. Listening is fundamental to our survival, and we engage all our senses to do so: hearing, smell, taste, touch, and sight. As actors, we are not merely "acting" but actively responding and listening to the world around us. Both performance and rehearsal arenas provide a space for listening, instinct, and spontaneity, creating an authentic lived experience for the performer.

So, how do actors effectively listen and respond to something they've heard a hundred times? How do they convince the audience that they're experiencing sights for the first time, even after multiple takes? Every actor has faced the challenge of a script feeling stale and overworked, so what can we do to avoid this situation? The answer may differ for each individual but from my experience, it's drawing upon techniques that aid spontaneity, presence, and in-the-moment creativity. Whilst the script does not change, the performance in every take should vary, even if only slightly. No moment can be the exact same as another and our job as actors is not to duplicate moments but to stay present and live truthfully. We must plan less, play more, trust ourselves, embrace our imaginations and our co-actor's offerings, and let go. If our preparation leads to firm and inflexible choices, we limit room for play, resulting in a lifeless performance. If we learn our lines in a set way (a planned delivery), then our voices become rhythmic and stale. If we doubt our ability and instincts, we try to control the scene by playing things "safe" and our performance lacks colour and variety. To truly listen, we must be fully present, which requires letting go of control, expectations, and judgement. How do we achieve this? The actor must work to strengthen both their acting technique *and* their mindset so that they can trust their decisions and abilities. If the actor doesn't work on building their own innate confidence, they will forever seek validation and approval from others and fear of judgement will restrain their performance. The actor must have unwavering faith in their abilities and approach their work fearlessly and with ultimate openness.

To be open is to be free of expectations of where the scene should go. It involves accepting offers from our scene partner and being flexible in our approach to the work. For this to happen we must trust both ourselves and those we work with unconditionally. We must embrace a collaborative mindset rather than thinking we have all the answers. Most students never fully achieve openness in their performance, often attempting to control the scene by delivering lines in a rehearsed and set way. Because of this, they fail to genuinely hear the words, intonation, body language, and attitude of their co-actor which means the pair work as solo artists instead of a duet. Sometimes, actors try to let go and stay present, but nerves and fear push them back into familiar delivery patterns they perceive as safer. In such moments, it becomes essential to lean into fear and trust ourselves to embrace the unknown. We must understand that faith in our ability comes from striving for honesty and presence in our performance, not perfection, enabling us to react instinctively and intuitively. Whilst you may have discussed and agreed with your director on line interpretations, it doesn't mean the lines should be delivered with the exact same timing, tone, and rhythm every time. There can be slight variations as the moment allows. Openness involves being flexible and working collaboratively with your scene partner and director, not independently.

I've worked on sets where directors have changed things on the day, such as adding scenes or making script edits, or had different visions for certain scenes conflicting with my own. 'I've also had co-actors deliver lines in ways that were unexpected which meant I was required to adjust my performance to align with theirs. My character's intentions, beliefs, and objectives remained the same, but my delivery adapted to harmonise with the other performer. If we are open and flexible, changes can be incorporated with ease and minimal discomfort, allowing the creative process to flow.

I hear you, don't worry. As easy as it sounds, I know that it's not that simple. Acting is an art form that often places performers in high-stress situations, where they must deliver their best work under immense pressure. The pressure to remember lines, intentions, the director's notes, and ultimately not make mistakes is immense. Actors feel this pressure, and it can lead to the release of cortisol which can trigger an amygdala hijack. The amygdala hijack compromises the pre-frontal lobes (responsible for working memory) and triggers a fight, flight, or freeze response. Whilst this danger response was extremely useful for humans in the past, it now arises in less useful moments, particularly for actors. How can we listen effectively when we can't think straight? How can we trust ourselves to remember lines when our working memory is compromised? How can we react instinctively when our instincts urge us to run or freeze? This is where emotional intelligence comes into play.

As actors, we must take the time to understand ourselves, recognise our triggers, and learn how to manage our emotional responses. Emotional intelligence starts with self-awareness, and mindfulness plays a significant role in developing this practice. Our mind and body work together to generate emotional responses, and if the emotional response that arises is unhelpful, then it's up to us to create a new one. Useful in-the-moment strategies include breathing exercises to regulate our breath, power stances to encourage confidence, mindfulness techniques to foster presence, and positive self-talk to cultivate confidence. Section Two of this book will delve into mindfulness and self-belief in greater detail.

TASK

1. Practice attentive listening with all your senses when interacting with others.
2. Explore different environments, such as the busy city, the woods, and a place you've never been before. Listen to the sounds and sensations around you. How do these environments make you feel?

3. Avoid planning the exact delivery of your lines. Understand your character's motivations but remain flexible in your delivery. Be a duet not a solo artist.

An actor's instinct and intuition lie at the heart of their craft. However, from a young age, we are taught to silence our conflicting opinions, remain "polite", suppress emotions, and avoid challenging the status quo. As we get older, these restrictions become ingrained in our bodies and minds as learnt behaviours. Essentially, we have been trained to hide ourselves and our emotions from the world. Adhering to the numerous social norms and restraints of the twenty-first century can leave us feeling straight-jacketed and unable to access parts of ourselves we have worked unconsciously to conceal.

These learnt behaviours give rise to "cognitive biases", which are systematic errors rooted in our experiences that influence the decisions we make. These biases often revolve around the need to conform, the desire for acceptance, and the aversion to change. As you can imagine, these biases make our job as actors challenging, as we start prioritising fitting in over instinctual work. Humans have forgotten how to listen to their instincts, emotions, and gut feelings. We have been primed to listen to the voice of society out of fear of being outcast or rejected. This governing voice dictates our actions and thoughts, permeating our way of life and, unfortunately, feeding into our acting.

I met the most wonderful friend in Drama School who really struggled to let go and listen to her instincts as an actress. Raised by two nurses, she was taught not to drink too much, and not to lose control. She was overly cautious about everything, often shying away from taking risks out of fear of failure. This significantly impacted her work as an actress. She struggled to let go, felt the need for rigid control, and often ignored her instincts. Over the following years, she consciously worked on relaxing a bit more in her daily life, silencing the inner voice that said "no".

She gradually released the unnecessary restrains and gained self-trust, leading to a newfound sense of freedom in her acting. By courageously taking new risks and embracing the unknown, a new habit was engrained within her – one that fostered self-trust, spontaneity, and freedom.

TASK

1. Do you trust yourself enough to let go? If you struggle to trust yourself, how can you work on building it?
2. How can you encourage spontaneity in your life?

We often feel bound by the need to be accepted by society, and as a result, we go to great lengths to fit in and be liked. Let's face it, no one likes being judged. When we sense judgement, anxiety happens. We become afraid of what others think, of making mistakes, of not fitting in, and of being ostracised. This separation from others often leaves us feeling anxious, and it is this anxiety that leads actors to choose a safer, limited performance style – one that is likely to be accepted by others.

Individuals may fear that their performance will be "too big" or "too out there", causing them to deny and suppress their instincts, all in the name of maintaining a "natural" performance. However, if we allow our instincts and intuition to guide us, something unexpected and exciting may unfold during the performance. For some individuals, particularly those who prefer to have control, this is a risk they are unwilling to take. Consequently, freedom is compromised, and conformity and acceptance take precedence. There's an internal judge in every person's mind – an inner voice that fills us with doubt and compromises our self-belief. When actors listen to this judge and accept its offerings, they are unlikely to take risks; instead, they become controlled, monitored, and debilitated. They fall back on the rehearsal, the safe bet, the planned performance, and, in turn, the performance lacks life and spark. If we are to encourage unique and in-the-moment performances we must release the need for absolute control and acceptance from others and quieten the noise of the internal judge.

TASK

1. Can you notice when your own internal judge raises its head? Reflect on the fears and insecurities that arise from the internal judge. Write them down and challenge them individually. Create a more empowering thought for each insecurity.

2. Celebrate your wins rather than focusing on your faults. What is positive about your performance? What are your strengths? Get into the habit of writing these down and voicing them.

3. Approach your performance with the intention of serving the script, of collaborating rather than focusing on what you think the audience, director, or casting director wants. Trust yourself.

4. Make a list of all the positive qualities that make you unique and how you stand out.

As an acting coach, I've often witnessed actors hesitate after initially following their instincts in a scene. They retreat out of fear, worried that taking a risk might make them look foolish. This feeling stems from deep-seated doubt, fuelled by a lack of self-belief. It typically arises when the actor is not fully present but preoccupied with the audience's thoughts and judgements. Once doubt creeps in, fear takes hold – fear of losing control, fear of looking stupid, fear of getting it wrong, fear of being judged. Fear limits our instinctual responses, making us less likely to take risks. Our brain is wired to protect us and will ultimately do anything to keep us out of harm's way. Instead, we must strive to override fear, ground ourselves, and remain present so that we can listen to our bodies, connect with our emotions, and trust our gut. That gut feeling, often ignored, needs to be reawakened. I've heard that apple cider vinegar helps, so I'm necking that every day. But apart from that, it's a matter of practice which means reconnecting to yourself and leaning into the unknown.

Most humans crave acceptance, control, and validation, largely due to the extensive testing and grouping we experienced growing up. However, for an actor to thrive, they must set aside those concerns and embody "freedom techniques". These techniques empower actors to embrace fear and uncertainty. I suggest practising freedom techniques in both real life and in performance. To experience more freedom in your personal life means stepping out of your comfort zone, and doing things you wouldn't normally do. It means living consciously, daring to be vulnerable and fully committed. It involves pursuing the things you've always wanted to do but have held back from. It means granting yourself permission to feel and openly discuss your feelings and emotions. It means confronting fear head-on instead of avoiding it. It means being more vulnerable and listening to your gut. It means being comfortable with failure with a sole focus on growth. It requires listening to your mind, body, and soul to feel connected to your true self and to act in alignment with that. So let's get one thing clear, I'm not encouraging anything illegal here or giving you an excuse to shout at that idiot who's been annoying you for some time – those impulses are best kept in check. However, I am asking you to raise your awareness of the impulses that you may have been suppressing. Developing an awareness of the instinctual drives that guide us in life will not only transform your approach as an actor but also enhance your overall happiness.

TASK

1. Increase awareness of your internal voice and cognitive biases that influence your behaviour. Take note of instances when you hesitated to speak or act, feared change, suppressed your instincts, or buried certain emotions. Often we deny ourself

our voice for fear of how it will affect others, notice when you are doing this and how that feels in the body. Becoming clear about these patterns will heighten your awareness of your instincts and intuition when they arise.

2. Start to notice the internal changes that occur in the body, practicing mindfulness can help with this. See the chapter on this.

3. Challenge yourself to act on your intuition and gut instinct.

4. Challenge yourself to do something out of the ordinary every day. Take a different route to the shop, wake up to a new song, or call a friend who you haven't spoken to in a while.

5. Regularly do things that scare you. This could be anything from learning a new skill, attending a new class, taking a new course, or asking someone out.

6. Learn to trust yourself by not always seeking constant advice from others. Trust your ability to know what is right for you and your ability to learn if failure occurs. The answers you seek can be found within you.

How do we get comfortable with discomfort for long-term gain? This is one of the biggest challenges we face because most of our lives are tailored around making us more comfortable. We are a society obsessed with making things more comfortable and easier; Deliveroos, Ubers, cars, online shopping, and practically everything you see have been created to make life easier for us. We have been primed for comfort and ease and have lost sight of delayed gratification. People want results now and they want the easy way. However, when it comes to managing our emotions and leaning into fear there is no simple solution. Our ability to sit in discomfort or embrace discomfort not only enhances our resilience but also our emotional regulation and self-trust. So what could we do to encourage this? It could mean going for an early morning run at 6 a.m., taking a cold shower, changing your commute route, brushing your teeth with your non-dominant hand, or talking to a stranger. Stepping outside of your comfort zone in your everyday life means that you will feel more comfortable doing this in all areas of your life as you start to feel more empowered and alive. As humans, we crave the familiar because it gives us a sense of certainty, which is essential for our survival. We're not always fond of too much uncertainty, especially in moments when we feel stressed. Therefore, we must practice embracing discomfort and apply this to our acting work. When you allow spontaneity into your performance and step away from the planned performance, guess what happens? It feels really bloody uncomfortable. Why? Because you're stepping into the unknown without a safety net. But by taking the necessary steps to move out of our comfort zone, we can engage rather than retreat, feel excited rather than fearful, and fight rather than freeze. The more we practice, the more we can manage our stress hormones in fearful situations and open ourselves to new experiences and opportunities.

Perspective shifts and reframing will help you lean into fear. How can you change the way you think about things to feel better about a situation? Are you nervous or excited? Which perspective is more useful? I would argue that many actors accept the fickleness of the industry because it offers the possibility of life-changing experiences overnight. We thrive on the uncertainty but more so the opportunity to "make it". The dopamine rush we experience when playing a slot machine or the lottery is probably not too dissimilar to the one we experience when auditioning within the acting industry. The acting industry, with all its uncertainty and opportunity, makes us feel alive and excited. For me, changing my perspective on nerves transformed my approach to auditioning. I reframed how I saw my nerves. Instead of seeing them as debilitating and something to be fearful of, I accepted them and began to see them as a sign of being excited for what was to come. Nerves became evidence of my enthusiasm to share my work and collaborate. I stopped worrying about getting it wrong and focused all my energy on enjoying the process, living truthfully, and sharing my knowledge and talent. My energy was directed towards growth and resilience rather than solely winning the part. As a result, I went into each audition thereafter with a hunger and drive stronger than ever before. I didn't fear my nerves when they arose but accepted them and actually grew to like them. They made me feel alive. How can you look at things differently to work for you and not against you?

My next piece of advice may horrify you. It horrifies me, too, but I assure you it will be an effective tool for building confidence, managing stress, listening, and staying present. Are you ready? Act in front of family and friends and show them your work or share it on social media. Most actors fear performing in front of people that they know, especially people they care about. Why? Because these people are those we least want to be judged by. We want those we love to accept us and feel pride towards us, so the fear of being shamed in front of a parent or friend is much more scary than the fear of being shamed in front of a stranger. Many actors I coach hate it when I ask them to share their work for various reasons. Some fear that others will perceive their acting as bad, whilst others fear the judgement of being labelled an "aspiring actor". Many also fear that sharing their art may be seen as a form of arrogance. Regardless of what the fear is, hiding your talent from the world will not serve you. Once you begin revealing your work to those you love, something magical happens. You start to take ownership of your work and care less about what others think, understanding that it ultimately doesn't matter. You will never be accepted and adored by everyone, so why tailor your life for others to snuff you anyway? We cannot allow the fear of others' potential judgement to hold us back from achieving greatness and living our dreams. Remind yourself, who are you living for? Who deserves the power over your choices and your success?

Start acting for yourself, not for others. Start living for yourself, not for them. Practice performing in front of others at every opportunity you can. Take classes, hire a mentor, do scenes with your partner, friends, and family. Practice, practice, and then practise some more. Share your work on social media, TikTok, or wherever suits you. Set up a YouTube channel or even perform on the streets if you like. Show everyone what you are capable of. This will allow you to embrace fear and face nerves with confidence as you begin to accept your talent and capabilities. When your confidence is high, you can commit wholeheartedly and stay present.

Remember, an actor who is present and in the moment creates a performance filled with life. When we start to listen to our instincts, embrace fear, and trust ourselves, we stress less about lines but rather immerse ourselves in the action and become fearless courageous performers. An unpredictable actor is a wonderful actor to watch. The best performances are the ones that feel instinctual, brave, and honest.

TASK

1. How can you reframe your perspective to work in your favour? Consider shifting your mindset about auditions and performances. Can you view auditions as rehearsals, where you have the opportunity to explore and refine your craft? Can you reframe nerves into excitement?
2. Show your work to your family.
3. Share your work on social media.

14. Imagination

Submerging ourselves into a scene is not always an easy task, especially when working in genres like horror, sci-fi, or fantasy. Imagination plays a crucial role in conveying a convincing story to our audience, and we must work hard to keep it active. So, how do we activate our imaginations?

There are various techniques in this book designed to activate your imagination, but the first piece of advice is to research, research, and research some more. We must understand the life of our character and the world they inhabit. If your character has a specific job, research what the job entails. If they live in an environment dissimilar to your own, for example, on a spaceship or even just near a beach, immerse yourself in videos and materials that capture those circumstances. A film set in a different time period requires a deeper understanding of the traditions, cultural differences, and prevailing ideologies of that era. Close your eyes, imagine the world, and imagine living in it. Leave no aspect unexplored, from clothing choices to personal beliefs, take your imagination to your character's world.

Working with our imagination allows us to wholeheartedly believe in the world of the scene. Think about observing a child playing with a dollhouse, completely in awe; nothing can take them out of that world. They imagine everything with such precision, it feels incredibly real to them. Or when a child pretends to throw a Pokémon Ball to release a Charizard, we can see the realness of that imagery in the child's eyes. We are taken on that journey with them because they fully commit and believe. As we grow older, we are encouraged to reign in our imaginations and to live in the "real world". We are taught to focus on work, to be practical, and to avoid getting distracted by unrealistic visions. However, we need to remember what it was like to be a child. What it was like to play, to imagine, and feel free. We need to release the constraints we've imposed on ourselves and learn to let go.

TASK

1. Reconnect with your childlike self. Reflect on your past and remember what it was like to be a free-spirited kid. What did you love to do?
2. Write down some childhood memories where you felt truly free.

In order for us to connect to our character, we must open our hearts and activate our imagination. We must try and understand their lived experience. When you receive a scene, it's important to try to relate to it in any way possible. Is the action in the scene or situation something you have experienced? If not, have you encountered something similar? Take the time to comprehend the character's world, their everyday life. How does it shape their beliefs, motivations, and behaviours? Perhaps they believe that they are invincible and always on a winning streak, or maybe they perceive life as constantly throwing obstacles in their way. Their beliefs in the piece hold significance, and we must be specific in exploring them to infuse our performance with intricate nuances. We are all governed by the beliefs we have, whether we like it or not. Our beliefs affect every decision we make because they affect what we feel is possible for us. Therefore, it is imperative we explore our character's beliefs and imagine how these beliefs govern their lives.

TASK

1. Take the time to really explore your character's journey and find points of relatability.
2. Envision what a typical day looks like for your character.
3. Identify the beliefs your character holds. What is holding them back? What beliefs do not serve them? Do they hold any conflicting beliefs (most of us do).

How can activating our imagination help us produce non-stereotypical characters, ones with gravitas and nuances? In one of my workshops, we explored this. I handed out the script to the students. It was fairly vague and involved a killer and a detective. They had two weeks to prepare, and all the students seemed very excited. On the week of showcasing their scenes most of the students playing the role of the killer really struggled to embody their characters. Their portrayals relied heavily on stereotypical choices and lacked authenticity and uniqueness. Their character physicality and mannerisms presented "evil" but did not feel evil. It all felt like an act, like the actor wasn't in their body.

Many of the students playing this role struggled because of their lack of understanding of the character. When I asked them about their characters' reasons for murdering people, most of them responded with answers like "because they enjoy it" or "because they are psycho". Some students even told me they didn't know. Unfortunately, these answers didn't allow the actors to connect with their characters because they stemmed from their own judgements rather than the characters' lived perspectives. Consequently, their performances became representations of what they thought a psycho would be, rather than exploring the motivations and beliefs that could drive such behaviour. The students hadn't tapped into their imagination to develop a backstory or delve deeply into their characters' motivations and personal history. They hadn't explored their characters' insecurities, fears, or beliefs, and this lack of investigation and imagination consequently led to a lack of clarity, variety, and gravitas. Every individual has a rationale for their behaviour, the "bad" ones don't see themselves as evil at all. Everyone is acting and fighting for something, and it is the actor's responsibility to locate, understand, and embrace that something.

TASK

1. Consider your character's motivations behind their decisions.
2. Consider your character's insecurities and the reasons behind them.

When an actor's imagination is activated, the performance will be filled with subtleties and intricacies. The actor will explore the relationship between the character's history and attitudes, and the impact this has on their behaviour and physicality. Using this knowledge, they may find they alter the way they walk or stand and the way they use their voice in terms of rhythm and tone. The actor who harnesses a strong imagination will understand deeply how their character feels, they will know if the character holds resentment, bitterness, or fear. They will understand how this affects the way they perceive others as well as the way they perceive themselves. Someone with a negative self-image, riddled with insecurities and doubt, will interact very differently to a character who holds a positive self-image and beams with confidence. By thoroughly exploring the character's view of the world and their belief systems and insecurities, the actor gains a clearer understanding and insight into who their characters really are.

Character research, in combination with imagination, allows actors to creatively explore the different ways that a character may stand, move, or talk. For instance, I naturally speak with speed and have a heightened energy, so playing a character with high status and gravitas perhaps requires me to adjust my mannerisms to suit. This may involve slowing down speech and movement, improving pronunciation, or moving more deliberately. Researching other people who hold similar personality traits to the character you're playing can be helpful, whether they are real people or fictional characters from films. This research, coupled with commitment, courage, and activated imagination, can inspire creativity in embodying the character's physicality during performances. Always try to take it back to the character's lived experience. For example, Matthew McConaughey who plays Ron in *Dallas Buyers Club* adjusts his physicality to represent a man who has faced extreme hardship and alcohol addiction. We literally see the weight of these addictions on the physicality of Ron. Ron is slouched, hunched over, his hair is overgrown, and he is very thin. He talks slowly and walks with a swagger. This air of attitude clearly masks his inferiority complex. Both the weight of his life and the way he perceives himself affect his physicality.

TASK

1. How do your character's motivations, background, and beliefs affect their physicality and mannerisms?

2. How does your character perceive themselves? Do they have a positive or negative self-image?

3. What opinions does your character hold towards other characters?

4. Consider how your character walks, talks, and moves. How has their history and life shaped their physicality? For example, if they have experienced a difficult or challenging life, how does it manifest in their posture and movements? If they suffer from a drug or alcohol addiction, it may be reflected in a hunched walk. If they are anxious, they may walk and talk faster.

One area we have yet to explore is how we can utilise our imagination to enhance emotional connection. I remember teaching a class with a script that centred around an argument between a husband and wife. Two of the students came to me as they were really struggling to emotionally connect to the script. They had done their research and understood the context, beliefs, and motivations of their characters, but their performance still lacked spark and intensity. The students had created strong objectives and broken down their script to a professional standard, yet it all felt on one level – something was missing.

I invited the students to do a couple of Stanislavski exercises: emotion memory and "magic if". For the emotion memory exercise, I asked the students to try to remember a past argument that was particularly upsetting. I encouraged them to explore how it felt, how it affected their body, and the way they held themselves. I asked them to explore this memory a little deeper with their eyes closed. After a few moments, I stopped the exercise, mindful of not letting the actors dwell on past trauma or risk playing the memory rather than the story within the script.

Next, we explored Stanislavski's magic if exercise. I asked the students to imagine truly being in their character's shoes. How would it feel? What would be their inner turmoil? Once again, the actors closed their eyes to explore this. I encouraged them to look beneath the surface and consider the deeper anxieties of their characters – their deepest and darkest fears. I asked them to contemplate contrasting emotions and avoid making one layered and stereotypical assumptions about their character's inner life.

After our imagination work, the students performed again, and to their delight, a connection was made. The actors' imagination aided in an emotional connection, immersing them in the life of the scene and actively participating in its creation, rather than merely imitating it. Often we can get locked into the theory and overlook emotional connection. We as humans act based on our emotions therefore it is imperative that we work with our imagination to truly understand and feel what emotions our characters are going through.

TASK

Consider utilising these techniques to improve your imagination and connection to your characters:

1. **Emotional memory:** A Stanislavski approach where a memory from the actor is utilised to recreate an emotion their character is feeling.
2. **Substitution:** A technique developed by Uta Hagen where the actor revisits a past similar experience that relates to the circumstances in the scene.
3. Explore Sanford Meisner's work on **Living Truthfully Under Imaginary Circumstances**, which provides valuable insights on this topic.

The next task box contains a variety of techniques to stimulate your imagination. Use the ones you find useful and disregard any that seem less effective. One tool I haven't covered in this section of the book is Stanislavski's "the method" approach. With this approach, the actor essentially embodies the character and lives as that character for a set period of time, sometimes for extended durations. Whilst this approach can be effective, it can also be quite harmful to our own psyche if practised for prolonged periods. Our brains are malleable and can grow and rewire. If we feed our brains negative thought patterns, there is a chance that they may stick.

From my own experience, playing a low mood character for an extended time can impact me for a few days after filming. It's important for me to dissociate from that character between scenes whenever possible and once we have finished shooting. If a specific emotional state is required for the duration of the day I may choose to stay "in the zone", particularly between takes; however, I must stress the importance of dissociating between you and the character where possible, especially post-filming.

Having a post-filming strategy is fundamental for your mental health as an actor. This may involve socialising, changing your physiology, going for a run, listening to upbeat music, doing something fun, or hanging out with family. Each actor should find their own unique way to bring themselves back to their current world. Some actors who have used the method have experienced taking on their character's emotional state and have struggled with their mental health during and after production. It's important to remain cautious with this approach, being mindful of your own mental health and reflecting on whether this practice poses a threat to your emotional well-being. Acting is a job and should be treated as such. Your mental health is not worth compromising when other acting technique tools are available.

TASK

Imagination tasks.

1. **Create character diary entries or poetry.** This will help you immerse yourself in the character's world and understand their daily lived experience.

2. **Research.** Immerse yourself in the character's social, historical, and cultural history.

3. **Watch films, TV shows, footage, or read books on topics that cover similar subject matters or have similar storylines.** This will offer inspiration and a clear understanding of the topic or genre you are working with.

4. **Go into nature.** Close your eyes and imagine your characters. Consider your character's world and their journey in the great outdoors. Nature has been proven to open doors for creativity. I often find that I am most creative when walking amongst nature.

5. **Do your homework** and break down your script into actions and objectives. Map the character's journey effectively.

6. **Improvise** the scene with your scene partner. Improvise other "made up" scenes. (See Chapter 16 on Improvisation)

7. **Practice empathy.** At the heart of acting is empathy and gaining a deep understanding of what your character is going through. Practice empathy on a daily basis. Try to imagine

being in other people's shoes and what that experience would be like for them.

8. **Connect emotionally.** Imagine the emotions that your character is going through and how they feel in the body.
9. **Learn about human psychology.** Learn about humans, the brain, and how we think and operate. This will help you understand what motivates your character and allows for a more imaginative approach.
10. **PLAY. Have fun!** Try the script in different ways. Consider the opposite. Enjoy the process and embrace all exploration areas in the rehearsal room.

15. Human Psychology

I believe that it is important for every actor to become aware of the basics of human psychology and the brain. We need to understand why our characters may behave and react in the way they do. As an actor, I encourage you to be curious about how the brain works. I advise most of my students to read up on emotional intelligence and human psychology to develop a basic understanding of this area.

TASK

1. Read *Emotional Intelligence* by Daniel Goldman.

One useful thing we can do in our preparation for a role is to consider deeply the true motivations of our character and how these link to our basic needs. We all have needs that must be fulfilled and Tony Robbins, an author, coach, and philanthropist who specialises in human psychology, suggests in his book, *Unleash the Power Within,* that these needs include certainty, uncertainty, significance, connection, love, growth, and contribution.

I would add that many people are also searching for acceptance, peace, and balance.

The hustle and bustle of life often means that we do not always operate in the most productive ways. Many of us are addicted to stress and struggle to switch off, whilst others struggle with motivation and change. This leaves us feeling restless and irritable, longing for peace and balance. We also constantly strive for acceptance, living in fear of rejection and being outcast by a particular group or person. We live in a society where comparisons and likes on social media have become ways to validate ourselves and others. We must, if we are to understand our characters' lived experiences, consider how their psychology affects the decisions they make, the beliefs they have, and the behaviours they exhibit.

Humans move towards things they believe will bring them happiness and away from painful experiences that may cause harm. Every experience shapes the way humans interact in life. The brain is constantly trying to hold onto information that can potentially save our lives or prevent us from experiencing pain. For example, if your character went through a horrible break-up where they felt financially, emotionally, and mentally vulnerable, they may approach the next relationship with caution. If the character is someone who seeks power and control, perhaps they felt powerless in the past and are attempting to reassert themselves. If a character struggles in relationships and always leaves before getting too deep, perhaps they struggle to trust others. What do your character's actions, attitudes, behaviours, and beliefs reveal about them?

TASK

Ask yourself these five key questions:
1. Which human needs have not been met for your character? Certainty, uncertainty, significance, connection, love, growth, contribution, acceptance, balance, or peace?

2. How have their past struggles and torments shaped their attitude?
3. What truths do they hold onto due to this?
4. What is your character innately longing for? (They will move towards this.)
5. What are they scared of or what has caused them pain in the past? (They will move away from this.)

16. Improvisation

Improvisation requires little preparation and is a spontaneous art form that also helps to activate the imagination. Within improvisation, there is no script and usually a very basic scene set-up. A stimulus is given, and the actors work with it to create a scene. Each actor will feed off of the other, allowing for a spontaneous, unplanned scene. It's a way for us, as actors, to access our imagination much more freely without the limitations of a script.

When we improvise, we aim to be truly present and in the moment. The lack of a script makes this process easier. It is essential that we try to think less and focus only on listening and responding so that we react with honesty and integrity. Many actors can often overthink their scenes, reluctant to let go and trust themselves. Improvisation is one tool that will help actors become active listeners, more spontaneous, and more trusting in their own instincts.

Improvisation is often feared by many actors as nothing is planned and anything is possible. This lack of control makes an actor nervous as they must open themselves up to uncertainty and possibility. It is for this reason that we must move through any resistance towards improvisation. We need to work with techniques that explore risk and spontaneity because these enrich every performance. Improvisation can often be seen as a comedy art form, and for this reason, many actors put too much pressure on themselves to be entertaining or funny instead of reacting instinctively and using their impulses. The actor's desire to entertain, please, indulge, and serve others rather than serve the moment becomes evident during improvisation. Improvisation reinforces the lesson that an actor's job is to serve the story.

When improvising, we avoid thinking to allow our instincts and impulses to take over, encouraging spontaneity. We must attempt to let go of any fear or expectation of what the scene could be or should be and allow things to take their course organically. Improvisation can be used in various contexts, including auditions, within the rehearsal process, and sometimes even during performances.

There are some key rules within improvisation. The first rule is that we do not block scene partners but remain open to the offers they bring. For example, if two people are standing at a bus stop (Character A and Character B), and A asks B for some money to start the improvisation, if B responds by saying they cannot give A money but there is a well across the road with lots of money within it, A should not block the offer. Blocking is a refusal to accept the offer being made. If A responds with "No, there isn't a well", that would be a block. Blocks hinder the progression of the improvisation, requiring both parties to work harder. A better response that would help the improvisation develop might be, "Oh, wow, could you help me find it? I heard that it's quite dangerous over there." This response accepts the offer and also introduces a new offer, moving the improvisation and story forward. The improvisation then starts to take a life of its own, with more ease, excitement, and imagination.

TASK

Consider these questions:
1. What is a block?

2. What is an offer?
3. Why is it important that we avoid blocks and make offers within improvisation?
4. Consider why improvisation is a useful tool for acting technique. What does it encourage?

Improvisation can also be a great tool for developing scenes as it allows an actor to explore the character's journey in more detail and depth. Using a scene from a script, we can take the key beats and then create an improvisation around those beats. This can often encourage a greater actor and character connection as we focus less on lines and more on the character's lived life, thoughts, and journey. When we are not fixated on the lines, we can speak freely, which often encourages a stronger emotional connection to our characters.

Improvisation is a useful tool to explore character development and relationships. We can create improvisations that encourage us to consider our characters' journeys and the relationships that they have within the script. For example, we could create improvisations based on how two characters met, fond memories the character has (wedding day, new job, first date), or a character's daily morning routine. We could also use hot seating to explore the types of things that our character might say and the way they might talk, move, and think. Hot seating is where an actor responds to a series of questions in character. The possibilities for improvisation are endless. I suggest that most actors practice improvisation as part of their continued craft and development. Viola Spolin's *Theatre Games* and Keith Johnstone's *Improvisation* explore improvisation much more deeply. If this subject is of great interest to you, I highly recommend researching these practitioners. It is good to be aware that auditions may sometimes ask for an improvised scene; this happens regularly in commercial auditions as most commercials are not dialogue-heavy.

TASK

1. Hot seat your characters. Ask friends and family to question you and answer the questions in character. Alternatively, you can record questions on your phone and then answer the recorded questions in character.
2. Practise improvisations. Attend classes, improvise with a friend, or film an improvised monologue.

Improvisation is a fun medium to explore our characters with freedom and spontaneity. It can activate our imagination and help us to bring nuances and subtleties into our performance as new things often surface through this process. Improvisation is an incredible tool for an actor's growth in terms of both their mindset and their creativity. With practice, the actor learns how to embrace presence and spontaneity and resists judgement and self-consciousness, creating a more instinctual, committed, and playful approach to the work.

17. Commitment

Unquestionable commitment in performance comes from a place of confidence and self-trust. In order to commit, you must feel that you have done the work, you must feel at the top of your game, and you must own the space that you are working in. There can be no room for doubt. Doubt creates tensions in the body, a nervous energy that can often creep into our mouths and jaws and inhibit us greatly. Doubt creates uncertainty, and this uncertainty is often centred around one underlying emotion: fear.

Fear is often the thing that holds us back. Fear of doing it wrong, fear of overplaying the drama, fear of forgetting the lines, fear of looking stupid, fear of not being good enough. Fear results in a very inhibited performance. Scared of how we will be received, we resort to playing it safe, aiming for naturalism. Naturalism is, of course, an incredibly important skill to uphold within the field of screen acting. However, many actors perceive naturalism as a stillness, a lack of facial movement, and a lack of emotion in general. Their attempts at naturalism often result in a very controlled and forgettable performance. It is my belief that true naturalism arises from an actor's confidence in owning their performance, staying present, and trusting their choices. A natural actor lives and breathes in the moment. They do not feel judged or self-conscious. They do not force or push too hard. They internalise their character's emotions and trust that the audience will see what they feel. They do not overcompensate or "show" in any way because they do not doubt their choices or their ability.

In order to achieve true naturalism and commitment, we must quieten the judgemental voice of the mind and instead work towards raising the voice of the character's mind, releasing all the depths of their nature: their wants, their desires, their vulnerability, what they have to lose, and their torments. This book has enabled you to unearth so many layers and depths of the characters that you play. What is the point in unearthing these layers if we are to hide under a plain mask? Don't concern yourself with what you look like or how others perceive you. Don't consider how your face is moving or what happened to your voice at that moment. Try to remove all thoughts of self-consciousness and focus on sharing and collaborating your interpretation of the character's story with the world. Stay present with your co-actor, listen, respond, and activate your imagination.

The hardest scenes for an actor to commit to are the ones where they feel they sacrifice their dignity. In other words, they feel stupid. Usually, when this happens, the actor will commit as if they are wounded. If a scene is taking you out of your comfort zone and you feel stupid, it is precisely at this moment that you should go full force because if you don't, I guarantee you *will* look stupid. When the director tells you to imagine that a monster has just eaten your sister and to react, if you do not fully commit, your performance will suffer.

I have watched this happen over and over again, in films and in lessons, where an actor has fallen into the trap of a wounded commitment, a commitment that was sacrificed for fear of looking stupid. I understand that your instinct is preservation from judgement, and I understand that you may feel vulnerable and exposed, but if you don't lean into the fear, you will sabotage your work as an actor. If you find a scene uncomfortable because it brings about self-consciousness, it is essential you override it.

One student was struggling with their own commitment in a scene. When we delved deeper, we found that it was the anger in the scene he was struggling with. Innately, this individual was a quiet guy and had a lot of judgement towards those who expressed themselves with anger and disdain, so much so that it actually affected his ability to play any character who "lost it". He said he was able to control and repress his own anger. He never felt it so if he was never angry in real life, how could he show it with his characters? I asked him to do the following things:

1. Avoid focusing on the emotion "anger" but rather the fire, fuel, and fight.
2. Consider the reason why his character was angry and behaved in the way that they did. What was happening underneath? What were their fears and insecurities? What was driving them to behave in that way? What did they want to achieve? Can he relate to that?
3. Consider a time when he fought for something and how that felt. How did he behave?
4. Consider a time he didn't get what he wanted and how that felt.
5. Consider a time in the past when he felt threatened and vulnerable.

6. Notice when things annoy him and how it initially feels so that he becomes more aware of that bubbling, stomach-turning sensation when anger or irritation appears. As actors, we must be able to access our emotions, even the ones we don't often show, becoming aware of when they raise (even just ever so slightly) their head.

7. Research how people behave when they are angry. What do they do with their body, with their voice?

8. Remove the judgement he has towards his character's behaviour and anger itself. When is anger a useful solution to a problem? Why do we have anger in the first place? Why do some people get more angry than others? What would that be like? What does he think causes this? How can he remove his judgement towards the emotion of anger?

9. Practise playing the characters that "lose it" repeatedly and have fun without judgement. To try it in various ways until he feels at peace with doing it.

10. Finally, I asked him to lose his expectation of where the scene must go. His focus was solely on presenting an emotion and fear of not being capable, rather than enjoying and immersing himself into the scene. To commit, he needed to release his expectations and instead focus on the character's journey and their internal struggles, and trust that the rest would naturally unfold.

To truly commit, you must confront the insecurities that hold you back. Fundamentally, you may fear judgement, failure, looking a fool, and not being good enough. However, it is essential to acknowledge that judgement is likely, as humans tend to judge, so worrying about it serves no purpose. Instead, focus your energy on being the best version of yourself. Understand that everyone will have their own opinions based on their lived experiences and perspectives. Trying to please everyone is futile. Overcoming these thoughts and alarm signals in the body is challenging, but with practice, you will get better. Challenge negative thoughts when they arise and shift your focus towards opportunities rather than fear. Change your perspective on nerves and reframe them as excitement. Focus on the present and the breath to calm the alarm in the body.

Lastly, do the work. If you don't understand why your character behaves a certain way, it will hinder your commitment. It is your job to fully understand your character's motivations. Consider the stakes for your character If they do not achieve their desires. What is at risk for your character? The previous chapters on imagination and emotional connection will help you with this process. You must feel a deep, internal emotional charge to truly grasp and understand your character's hardships and struggles. This level of connection can propel an actor into wholehearted commitment.

In a short film I starred in, I played a mother who discovers that her son has fatally beaten a close family friend whom he believed was a paedophile and had abused his little sister – my daughter. To prepare for this role, generating a real, organic emotional connection was crucial. One exercise that significantly helped both my emotional connection and my commitment was an imagination exercise. As I don't have children, I imagined how I would feel if this had happened to my little niece. I looked up the actors playing the other characters and used their images to visualise the sequence of events. Whilst saying the lines, I immersed myself in this imagined scenario. I considered what was at stake: my son going to prison, my friend's death, my daughter's abuse, the involvement of social services. I repeated this exercise several times, and certain words in the script became emotional triggers. The guilt I felt as a failed parent and the pain I felt at the loss of a friend were all rising within me. It wasn't a pleasant experience, but it created such a mark on me that I made a connection. We must be willing to explore unpleasant places to really understand our character's pain; we cannot shy away from this. When we connect to these pains emotionally and truthfully, our commitment intensifies drastically. Obviously as always make sure you do not sacrifice your own mental health. If a role triggers you negatively, it might not be the role for you. Instead, you may opt for working on healing that part of you so that next time you are equipped to handle such a role.

As an actor, commitment is essential. There's no room for ego, for self-criticism, or half-hearted performances. If you struggle with your imagination or your ability to emotionally connect, you must practise and improve on these skills. If you struggle with self-negative talk and self-consciousness, you must work on your confidence by working on your mindset and limiting beliefs, which we will explore later on. Remember to find the fun in the scene. Enjoy the journey, and don't obsess over looking like an idiot – the chances are if you do this, you will. Where focus goes energy flows. Instead, make it your goal to stay truthful and loyal to the script.

18. Vulnerability

Society has shaped a world where vulnerability is seen as a weakness. We are told by our parents not to cry, to be a big boy or girl. We are taught to stay strong, and that life is tough but we must get on with it. We bury our feelings so that we can carry on with our day and get the jobs that need to be done finished. We hide our emotions for fear of being seen as weak or damaged. We've become masters of hiding what we really feel because, let's face it, the more vulnerable we are the more likely we are to get hurt. We believe the less vulnerability we expose, the less likely we are to be judged, so we continue to conceal our emotions. As actors, the challenge lies in unearthing our character's vulnerability when we've trained our bodies to suppress it for so long. How can we become comfortable presenting such uncomfortable emotions?

The truth is, we all experience vulnerability at different points in our lives. Vulnerability makes us humans, and it's what helps us to connect with each other. We all understand the feeling of vulnerability, and when others around us display it, it resonates with us as well. Ironically, we tend to be much more open and compassionate toward others' vulnerabilities than our own. When a friend comes to us in need of help or emotional support, we offer our hand, yet we deny ourselves the same kindness, berating ourselves for feeling that way.

When we are openly vulnerable, we reveal a raw and honest part of ourselves that we perceive as weak, but others often see as strength. It takes massive amounts of strength to be openly vulnerable, and when we allow ourselves to do so, people are drawn to us. In our vulnerability, we are genuine, and others connect with us on a deeper level. They see our pain, our suffering, and they recognise a part of themselves that has also experienced similar challenges. People appreciate seeing humanity in others, and vulnerability represents just that. Therefore, it becomes crucial for our characters to be vulnerable so the audience can relate and warm to them.

Vulnerability helps create likeable, authentic characters and a gripping story that captivates the audience. It allows the audience to relate to the character's pain, fostering an emotional attachment to both the character and the story. As actors and storytellers, we want an interested and engaged audience – one that responds emotionally to what they see on the screen and becomes invested in the story. Vulnerability is what transforms "villains" into likeable characters whom the audience continues to watch and sometimes even root for, even when their actions are questionable. I often think of James McAvoy's character in *Split*, where he plays a character with dissociative identity disorder who embarks on a journey of kidnapping and harm. McAvoy skilfully tapped into his characters' vulnerabilities and insecurities, enabling the audience to empathise with a character who commits unspeakable acts. Another wonderful example is Joaquin Phoenix's performance as the Joker, which demonstrates how an outpouring of vulnerability can encourage an audience to root for the "baddie".

So, how do we access our vulnerability within performance? How do we allow ourselves to let go? Perhaps the first step is to understand ourselves better. To notice when we feel vulnerable in life and how we cope with it. What methods do we use to suppress or deny vulnerability? Pay attention to moments of fear and hurt and observe your defence mechanisms. Getting to know ourselves and identifying the situations that make us feel most vulnerable is crucial. Often, we suppress and hide our emotions, but in doing so, we lose the ability to express them. The more we understand ourselves, our triggers, and our patterns, the better equipped we are to use them to our advantage in our performances. Self-awareness and awareness of others' experiences will aid us in our quest to achieve vulnerability. Observe how people approach vulnerability, not just in real life but also in films. We must be curious about people and start to understand the way they work if we are to realistically portray them.

The next stage is to remove judgement from being vulnerable. It is acceptable to build walls, reject tears, and remain strong, but it is equally acceptable to feel vulnerable, cry, and allow ourselves to experience our emotions when we need to release them. We should not feel the need to mask these aspects of ourselves. Let go of judgement and allow yourself to feel what you feel. Additionally, delving deeply into your character without judgement can be helpful. Rationalise their actions and approach them with understanding, love, and compassion. If you have done the work laid out in this book, you should already know your character's fears within the scene, but can you go deeper? What is your character's biggest fear in life? What do they try their hardest to hide from the world? Are they scared of being alone? Of dying? Of not being accepted? Of financial instability? Lack of trust? Lack of confidence? These insecurities, the things we work so hard to conceal, are what the audience can connect with and relate to. By homing in on them, we can not only capture the emotional depths of our characters but we also create imperfect yet likeable characters that draw the audience in. If you struggle with vulnerability in performance, I suggest the following:

KEY ADVICE:

1. Do the work outlined in the book, particularly the imagination exercises.
2. Find a place in the script where your character feels vulnerable – usually a moment of fear, insecurity, or exposure. Consider what they are trying to hide; often, it can be found in the subtext (things that are unsaid).
3. Show your character compassion and understanding. Truly imagine what they are going through and the impact it has on them. Be kind to your character.
4. Become aware of any negative judgements you may have regarding emotional expression, and then reframe these judgements. Accept that everyone handles their emotions differently, including your character.
5. Stay focused on your character and their story at all times. Avoid making it about yourself.
6. Remind yourself of your character's fears and hopes.
7. Try not to force an emotion; instead, allow it to come through naturally.

19. Professionalism

Acting is no different from any other job when it comes to the requirement of maintaining professionalism at all times. Often, you will be working with the same people for extended periods, and the cast and crew may start to feel like family. However, this familiarity can sometimes lead to distractions on set, such as laughing and joking at inappropriate times or engaging in unprofessional behaviour that can slow down the filming process. It is crucial to uphold a professional and helpful attitude as part of your job description as an actor. Always be prepared, punctual, and available.

I have been on sets where actors were unwilling to step in for an eye-line or performed miserably during someone else's close-up. Such work ethic should not be praised. Be available for your fellow co-actors and the director, even if you are not in the shot, and give your best performance whenever possible. Just because it is someone else's close-up and you aren't in the shot, it doesn't mean you can leave unless explicitly instructed to do so. Assume your co-actor will need you unless otherwise stated. An actor's responsibility does not end when the camera shifts away from us. We still have a duty to support our co-actor in delivering an authentic performance. This approach is both respectful and courteous and demonstrates professionalism.

There may be times when you need to give 70 percent instead of 100 percent, for example, if the scene is emotionally charged and requires you to get upset. In this instance, it is understandable that you may not cry in your partner's close-ups because delivering a 100 percent performance in every take can be emotionally exhausting. However, it is essential to remain focused, energised, and dedicated to your scene partner. I once had a student who even started looking at a distraction outside the window during their partner's close-up. This kind of behaviour only harms your own work. If you do not provide your partner with an honest performance, their reactions will be compromised, and the performances will not align. Imagine how frustrating it would be for you if your partner did not support you during your close-up – eyes wandering, lacking commitment or honesty.

What if they pulled a strange face due to a noise from outside? Wouldn't all of this annoy and distract you? Do not separate your performance from the team's overall goal. You are a small part of a bigger project, so work together, keep a great attitude, and the project will shine.

I would advise limiting the use of mobile phones on set as they can cause distractions. I remember a situation early in my career whilst working on a short film. It was one my first professional experiences as an actress since graduation, and I was very excited. During one scene, the director said that I could relax as he was going to move in on close-ups of the other actor. Naively, I took this note to heart and without checking if the actor still needed me or my eye-line, I took out my phone and was smiling as I eagerly texted my friend an update. What I didn't realise was the other actor was still using me as an eye-line since it was his close-up. Once the actor had finished his close-ups, he came over and yelled at me, accusing me of being rude for using my phone and claiming it had distracted him from his performance. In that moment, I felt attacked, shocked, and very embarrassed. He had humiliated me in front of everyone. Whilst his approach may have been questionable, I knew deep down that he was right – I should have been more aware, professional, and available to him. The phone should not have been my focus; the job should have been my focus. Every job is a learning curve, and on that day, I learnt three important lessons:

1. To always be respectful and available for my fellow actors, even when I am not "technically" needed.
2. To be aware of my surroundings at all times on set and be less available to my phone.
3. To be open, honest, and kind. To ask for anything I need to enhance my performance and communicate with others respectfully, recognising that we are all working toward the same goal.

Throughout my career, I have asked other actors who have been dismissed by the director to stay on set to work with me. It helps with my performance and my eye-lines, and every actor has always been extremely happy to help. You must remember, though, that acting is mentally and physically exhausting. If the director releases the other actor, they may choose to leave, and we must respect their decision and be prepared for this outcome, just in case. There may be times when you have to perform without your co-actor, such as when they are not available on the shoot day or when working with child actors who have limited time on set. Acting under these circumstances can be challenging as you are essentially acting with a stand-in or no one. In such instances, immerse yourself in your imagination, maintain a clear eye-line, and remember your character's objective. Refer to the previous section of this book for guidance.

Unless stated otherwise, always be prepared. There may be long periods of waiting on set due to various delays, but don't let this derail you. Whilst it's good to socialise and get to know everyone in the green room, ensure that you're in the right frame of mind to work when you're called, whatever that means for you. Check your costume, touch up your makeup, use the toilet, and emotionally prepare yourself for the scene. If you've had downtime with other actors, practice your lines and delivery so you're ready when you step on set. For emotional scenes, you might want to create some distance from others to stay focused. Treat every opportunity on set as a chance to showcase not only your talent and ability, but also your teamwork, friendliness, helpfulness, positivity, and energy. In this industry, who you know is as important as what you know, and your success depends on building strong working relationships. Remember people's names, take the time to get to know everyone's role on set, and always be polite so that people remember you as great to work with.

However, whilst it's beneficial to be positive and good to work with, avoid being needy. Don't hound casting directors, agents, or people on set. Neediness shouts creepiness and won't help you land you the roles you want and deserve. Consider anyone you have met who gave off a needy vibe – did it make you want to work with them or give your time to them? Neediness is undesirable in a human, though for some reason it is entirely acceptable with dogs. Whether you're in a casting workshop, an audition, or on set, avoid being overly desperate to please. Instead, approach the situation as a collaborator who brings skills to share. Remember that each person involved has something the other needs – it's not a one-way transaction. Stay grounded, knowing that you bring talent to the table.

20. Attitude

Your behaviour and attitude can determine whether you are hired, recommended, or ever work again. It is a fundamental component that changes the way people perceive you. If you have a positive and welcoming attitude, filled with enthusiasm and optimism, you are on the right path to creating strong professional relationships. When working with my students, I create an arena where we can play. We improvise, don't take ourselves too seriously, and foster an accepting environment where everyone can have fun and explore. Whilst most of what you have read so far has been very serious and technical, there's an important aspect of an actor's craft that cannot be overlooked: the ability to play and act the fool.

My students often joke that certain classes were created solely for my amusement, and whilst yes, that is a by-product, the real reason is something beneficial to them. Truthfully, they would be shocked at some of the things I have had to do in audition rooms. Despite their comments, my actions and lesson plans are not designed to make a mockery of them, granted this can be entertaining at times. These lessons are designed to prepare them for anything, enabling them to let go of their ego and operate with complete freedom. I've gone to auditions where I felt like an absolute idiot and my pride took over, sabotaging my audition. My pessimistic and egoic internal voice said, "they are making me look stupid" or "this is ridiculous", so instead of delivering 200 percent, I gave 20 percent, accompanied by a pessimistic and arrogant attitude. This did me no favours and certainly didn't land me the job.

As actors, we are expected to improvise and commit intensely to any scenario. We cannot succumb to fear or surrender to ego, we must be able to commit to the craziest of ideas. With CGI, AI, and green screens, the actor's job has become more challenging than ever, and we have to be able to sell whatever the author envisions. There are stories set in other worlds with superhuman and extraordinary creatures. There are stories set in multiple dimensions, on different planets, and in different times. We may be asked to do the craziest things to make a shot work, and we must align ourselves with the film's vision. In one job, I was asked if I would be happy to be dragged by the legs with a rope (and safety gear) whilst a leaf blower blew in my face and I screamed for my life. I obviously agreed because, for me, this is all part of the fun. Now, this may sound absolutely bonkers to you, but if I didn't commit, if I let my ego and my pride hinder me, the outcome of that scene would likely have been a failure.

I'm not suggesting that you should accept anything inappropriate – absolutely not. Everyone deserves respect, and it's your prerogative to choose what you are comfortable with and to discuss it with the director. However, if you choose to commit to something and your ego gets in the way, there could be problems. If you're not prepared and committed to go into an audition and prowl like a tiger, scream like a child, or howl like a wolf, you won't land a role in *The Jungle Book*, *Scary Movie 10*, or *Twilight*. We must practise being prepared, passionate, committed, open, and honest with the team we are working with.

What many people don't realise is that getting a job in this industry is not solely based on talent, but also on who you are as a person. People connect with people, and if you are someone who throws themselves into the work and gets the job done, you will have repeated opportunities. Production companies will remember you, create roles for you, and you will establish strong connections and a great reputation. Throw yourself in, enjoy the playfulness of it all, and be prepared for anything. With that being said, if something is asked of you that makes you uncomfortable, you owe it to yourself to speak up.

In one audition, I was asked to wear a mouth guard throughout the entire scene for a role as a character whose face gets "stuck in the wind". This mouth guard I had watched get passed around every actor auditioning, but I was reassured that the bowl of liquid it was placed in (for only seconds before it was passed to me) had disinfected it. When I placed the mouth guard in my mouth it was impossible to even say the words that I had remembered, and I was met with sniggers from the casting team which threw me off entirely. In hindsight, I probably should have said something. Not only was it unhygienic, but it was also not made clear beforehand that this would be expected of me. I was young, eager, and perhaps a bit needy, which made it easier for people to take advantage of me, knowing the competitive nature of this industry. Remember that you should never feel pressured to do anything you are uncomfortable with. If something makes you uneasy in any way, always discuss it beforehand. If at any point during an audition or on set you feel unsafe or compromised, speak up openly and honestly. Handling professional relationships is an important part of your job as an actor. It is crucial to understand the boundaries of the professionals you work with and ensure they understand yours.

When you arrive on set, be pleasant and get to know the people around you. It is your responsibility to create a good, professional working environment, so be mindful of your energy and bring positivity and enthusiasm. Don't be late. Ask questions if you're unsure of anything, but also make sure you do your homework. Know your lines and make sure you put in the effort to support your scene partner, even when the cameras aren't on you.

21. Auditions

Auditions can crop up at any time and are often very last minute. Every audition is a priority once you have accepted it. The competition for auditions is fierce, and many actors would give anything to be in your position, so seize that opportunity. Success in this industry requires effort, time, and dedication. If you find yourself questioning your commitment to an audition, you need to reflect on whether this industry is truly right for you or perhaps it is highlighting to you where you see your career going. If you do not want to do theatre you might feel resistance to a theatre job. Be open to your agent about where you want your career to go. If there are other factors at play, such as other commitments, then discuss these openly with your agent or representative.

Self-tapes have become increasingly common, especially since the pandemic, which has made the audition process more accessible for actors. Ensure you have a proper self-tape set-up, including good lighting equipment (preferably two soft boxes), a decent camera (most phones will suffice), a camera stand, and a clear background. Try not to record the self-tape too many times, but make sure the final tape showcases your best performance. Whenever possible, make sure you adhere to the stage directions, and if you want to add a hint of costume or makeup, that's absolutely fine. Be mindful of your eye-lines, do not look directly into the lens unless you have been directed to do so. Your eye-line should be just off-camera. Try and get an in-person scene partner where possible. If you are struggling to locate one, a Zoom partner would be the next best option. Lastly you can pre-record the other person's lines but I would use this as a last resort.

The acting industry has irregular work, plentiful rejections, and can feel quite infuriating if you allow it. It may feel like everything is out of your control, and you may beat yourself up over and over again about the failures you believe you've encountered, especially during or after auditions. You must remember that the entire casting process and industry are fundamentally rooted in subjective opinions and individual motives. Everyone involved has their biases and desires for the project's success. Casting is highly subjective, and often people have specific ideas or individuals in mind when the project is commissioned. Factors such as suitability for the role, audience appeal, talent, appearance, working dynamics, connections, experience, and reputation all play a role in casting decisions. The director, producers, casting director, and writer must collaborate to ensure the casting process is a success.

Here is how generally (not always) how the process works:

1. The project is written and handed over to a production company and a director.
2. The director/production team will usually assign a casting director to help them with the casting process, occasionally this is done internally.
3. A casting brief (a character breakdown) is created for each character.
4. The casting director sends the casting brief to agents via online portals like Spotlight or Casting Networks.
5. Agents submit actors that they feel are suitable for the job by providing your online CV, which is initially seen as a thumbnail photo (your headshot).
6. The casting director selects the pictures they feel best represent the character. They then narrow down their initial picks

further by looking at credits, showreel footage, location, skills, and other variables. Casting directors and the director may also approach individuals they believe may fit the project. If it's a leading role, they may already have a particular actor in mind, making the process much quicker.

7. Audition invitations are sent out to agents, who then contact the fortunate actors who have been selected. The number of selections can vary significantly.
8. The actor is asked to either attend an in-person audition or submit a self-tape. Usually, the first stage is a self-tape, and if successful, the actor will be invited to an in-person audition. The director, casting director, and producers may all be involved in choosing the right candidate.
9. Additional auditions may be required, such as chemistry reads or screen tests, to assess how actors work together or how they look on camera.
10. The actor is confirmed for the role.

As you can see, this is a lengthy and exhausting process for everyone involved, and this is just for one role. Many of those invited to audition will get the rejection we all fear, and unfortunately, most of the time, all they will receive is silence. No feedback, no clear understanding of why they weren't chosen, no clear explanation of what they "did wrong" – just silence. The casting process can be a challenging journey for any individual, especially when it seems to repeat in a continuous cycle. Someone once told me that out of ten auditions, you'll get one, but in my experience, especially with the rise of self-tapes, that number can be significantly higher. The impact of the casting process alone can wreak havoc on our self-esteem and motivation. Some struggle to get auditions, whilst others face rejection after rejection. Understanding how the audition process works and realising how many other actors are in the same situation can bring some relief when the outcome is not what you wanted.

Every casting is sent out to several agents, and each agent submits actors they believe fit the bill. From this vast number of actors submitted – and I mean *vast*; we're talking hundreds and sometimes even thousands – only one person will get the role. This can be determined by a range of things such as appearance, sound, talent, popularity, and accent, just to name a few. The casting process is cut-throat, but it also gives you a massive opportunity to make your mark.

Auditions give you the space and time to showcase your talent. The rise of self-tapes has meant that more people can be seen, which means that the work of unknown individuals can now be watched. It also means, however, that more people are being invited to audition. Remember to approach auditions as a collaborator, not as someone inferior or subordinate to the job or the people in the room. Never forget your place inside that room. You are neither beneath or above anyone else, and your behaviour should reflect that. Actors often place casting directors and directors on a pedestal, creating unnecessary distance between us and them. A distance, I must reiterate, that they did not ask for. Their job is very similar to ours; they too must pitch for jobs, and there's also hefty competition. If you feel a power imbalance, it is your responsibility to address it. In the audition room, be mindful of any changes in your behaviour, responses, or nerves. Develop self-awareness so that you can intercept nervous chatter or awkward tension as they creep in. See the audition room as a place to share your work and talent. Ask questions, be curious, and enjoy the process, because if you don't enjoy it, there is no point.

Ensure that you prepare well: learn your lines, be courageous with your decisions, and greet everyone with warmth and professionalism. If you need to refer to your script occasionally, that's fine, but try not to rely on it, especially if it was sent to you days in advance. Do your homework! Research the production genre, the casting director, and the director. And, of course, don't be late. If you're going to a new location, give yourself extra time to be on the safe side. Lastly, have lots of fun. The more fun you have, the more enjoyable it will be for everyone. Trust yourself. You've got this!

22. The Techniques Concluded

Within this book, you have become acquainted with acting techniques that will help you develop as an actor and allow you to create strong, powerful, and diverse performances. Utilise the tasks as much or as little as you like. Remember that these techniques are tools to help you, and you may find some more useful than others. That's okay. Discovering your own personal approach to your craft is a fundamental part of the process, and each person's approach will be unique and tailored to what works best for them.

I have shared what has helped me and techniques I have seen help others, but there is no one-size-fits-all solution. Personally, I know that to immerse myself in a scene, I need to activate my imagination, connect with extreme empathy, continuously work on my belief systems, and do the deep inner character work. Substitution and emotional memory are useful tools to get me into my character's mood prior to filming, but ultimately do not work for me during the performance, as I become absorbed in Michaela's world, in Michaela's history. In my performances, I like to fully embrace my imagination and the here and now, singing a duet with my scene partner, actively listening to them and building from that connection. As you become more skilled and practised, you will learn what works for you and what doesn't, and that's where the excitement lies because once you find something that works, it feels like a breakthrough.

Keep learning, explore different approaches within this book, and try tools from other authors and practitioners. Have fun with the process. Throughout your career, it is your responsibility to keep reading, watching other actors, learning, and practising your craft. If you're not growing, you're stagnating, and when you stagnate, you are not at the top of your game. Stagnation leads to a lack of motivation, care, and engagement, all of which fundamentally lead to one thing: a lagging actor. There is limited space in this extremely competitive world for a lagging actor, so keep growing and keep embracing new challenges.

Throughout the book so far, I have interwoven mindset principles with the techniques to help you understand that your individual perspective and focus are intrinsically linked to your skill as an actor. The next part of this book will delve more deeply into mindset. Although I have placed the mindset section secondary, I do not consider it a secondary skill. I firmly believe that not only your technique but also your mind, thoughts, and perspective are massively responsible for your success in this wonderful but mad industry. I hope you enjoy it.

PART 2:

CREATING A POWERFUL MINDSET

The mind is very powerful, more than we can fathom. Consider the art of suggestion, which magicians and illusionists use to easily influence our thoughts and decisions. The placebo effect is another example that demonstrates the power of the mind. In medical trials, a sugar pill is sometimes used instead of an actual drug (unknown to the patients), and researchers observe how this affects the patients. Amazingly, the placebo effect accounts for over 20 percent of all successful results in these experiments. This underscores the influence of our belief systems and the mind itself. When we truly believe that something will work, when we truly believe in ourselves, it makes a difference.

It is crucial to be aware of what you feed your mind, as the subconscious mind will always accept it as truth. If you convince yourself that you don't deserve to be in the room, that you are not good enough, smart enough, talented enough, or rich enough, you will sabotage your chances of securing any role. Through personal research and exploration, I discovered the limitations I had imposed on myself and sought ways to overcome them. Books like *The Power of the Subconscious Mind* by Joseph Murphy and *Emotional Intelligence* by Daniel Goleman provided valuable insights. I realised that my own negative self-talk had held me back in so many auditions. I found I had an unconscious belief deep down inside of me that I never knew I had. My desire and my self-image were not aligned, meaning I would always sabotage my best efforts in acting. I held a belief I never even realised I had. Deep down, I believed that my working-class background and poverty-stricken history didn't align with the stereotypical image of an "actor", and I feared being exposed as an imposter. This realisation was a shock to me because on the outside, I projected something entirely different. I appeared confident and outspoken, motivating others to pursue their dreams and emphasising the importance of self-belief. However, internally, I lacked belief in myself. Years of studying self-development and NLP have enabled me to unearth these self-imposed limitations and I work daily to eradicate them.

It isn't as easy as just saying what you want to believe out loud. The subconscious beliefs you hold will always come through, despite the mask you put over them. Think of it as a cake. As a child, the base is formed – the sponge. The sponge is initially light, airy, and pure, but its strength is influenced by various factors, including our interactions with caregivers, our sense of safety growing up, and whether our needs were met. These factors determine whether we have a sturdy or weak base.

As we grow older, we add multiple layers of filling to the cake – our knowledge and belief systems. Whilst much of the filling is helpful and aids our understanding of the world, some weakens the cake's structure. This includes our caregivers' limiting views about the world and about who we are / what we are capable of, any limiting beliefs about social class, race, and culture that are present during the time of our upbringing, and other people's and our own harmful opinions of who we are. From all of these things our self-image, which shapes our understanding of where we fit and what is possible for us, is formed.

Insecurities, limitations, and weaknesses manifest, but as humans dislike showing weakness, we mask it with a front. We put on a show, pretend to be a certain way, and make excuses for not showing up the way we want to (but don't believe we can). This is the cake's icy, thick, and heavy glaze that looks pretty but harbours the weight of unconscious limitations, insecurities, and debilitating beliefs. Sooner or later, the cake's foundations won't be able to support the weight of the glaze and temperamental fillings and cracks will appear. These cracks manifest as self-doubt, self-sabotage, and essentially give away our inner struggles. We start to feel vulnerable, unstable, and emotional, and at this point, we have a choice: we can either repeat the glazing process, further masking, denying, and adding to the weight of insecurities, or we can acknowledge the need for intervention and restructuring. Restructuring requires time, energy, hard work, and resilience. It involves identifying harmful limiting beliefs from our past, reframing them, owning our insecurities, and accepting the things we've tried so hard to hide for so long. Hard truths and significant change don't come easy, but they are a small price to pay for long-term peace.

Changing your belief systems can be taxing. Many books, YouTube channels, and coaches offer various methods and approaches to help overcome internal obstacles and limitations. All these approaches focus on one primary aspect, managing and becoming more aware of our thoughts and our body's alarm systems. We must learn to regulate the body first so that we can regulate the mind. To change our thoughts and belief systems we must acquire the necessary skills to consciously catch the negative thoughts as they arise so that we can reframe and challenge them. This section of this book will help you unearth and challenge your own self-limiting beliefs. It will give you the tools and techniques to create a more positive self-image that aligns with your goals. It will also explore practical ways that you can enhance concentration, avoid distractions, stay present and motivated, and above all, live optimistically in an industry filled with rejection and uncertainty. So, let's begin.

1. Mindfulness, Focus, and Distractions

For individuals who struggle to maintain focus, you are not alone, and this next section may be of some use to you. The ability to stay focused is crucial for any actor. We are mostly self-employed, meaning that we have to spend time looking and pitching for work on our own accord. We must develop the skills to manage our time and our focus efficiently. You are a business. Your image is your brand, and it takes effort and persistence to make this brand visible, understood, and felt by others. Actors must be able to stay focused on the end goal and delay gratification, as most of the effort they put in today will not manifest until tomorrow. Films take years to be made, emails take weeks to be opened, and creating a brand and a reputation takes a lifetime of patience. The actors who succeed keep their eye on the ball at all times and have nurtured uncompromising focus. Goal setting, creating a strategy, holding yourself accountable, and staying consistent will aid you in your quest to stay focused.

Focus, however, isn't only essential in the day-to-day running of the actor's business but also a vital part of the actor's craft when on set. Distractions are bound to happen on set or during auditioning. They are inevitable. Both external factors and internal factors will challenge your focus. External factors are things that happen outside of us, for example, during a performance you might experience movement in the background, hear external noise, or receive an unexpected reaction from your audience or scene partner that could throw you off a little. Internal factors are things going on inside of you, nerves and spiralling negative thoughts of "messing up" are perhaps the ones you are most familiar with. Distractions WILL occur, believe me, and if you allow them to take hold, your performance will be compromised. Though frustrating, we can develop techniques to adapt to distractions.

First, we must understand what we can control and what we cannot. Having spent enough time on set, I know that some distractions can't be avoided, whilst others arguably can. For instance, a crew member laughing or snoring in the next room (yes, this has happened to me) can be avoided. A sheep making strange wailing noises in the next field or a bee buzzing around you continuously mid-scene (again, this has happened) arguably can't be avoided. What we need to learn is how to deal with those situations in a professional manner when they arise and how we can prevent them from happening again, if possible.

If you find yourself distracted on set by something that can be controlled, try to calmly and respectfully state your needs. An example of this might be people laughing loudly on set when you're trying to do a very emotional scene. This is something very easily remedied, and a professional set will understand the importance of maintaining the right energy so that the best work can be delivered. Days on set are long and tiring, so making sure the environment remains positive is essential. The set becomes like a temporary family – they have your back at all times, but occasionally, like any family, they may annoy you a little. It is crucial for us to remember that we're all a team, working towards the same goal to make something incredible. Don't fear speaking up and asking for something that will enable the shoot to go smoother or enhance your performance in the film – everyone wants this. However, avoid making unreasonable requests or becoming a diva. Bring a genuine, helpful, and mindful attitude to create a beautiful working environment and establish positive industry connections.

So, what about the distractions you can't control? First, let's consider why distractions happen. The human brain's first and foremost job is to keep us alive, so it's always on high alert for movement and danger. It's no surprise that we're drawn to distractions. Another aspect is the reward system in our brain, which pulls us toward things that draw the senses in. A noise, movement, smell – anything that our senses latch onto can potentially cause a distraction. So, how do we stop ourselves from succumbing to such distractions? As with everything, focus is a skill that can be developed, but it takes time and energy.

Instead of dwelling on the distraction (and the internal dialogue that follows, the internal distraction), we must redirect our focus to something more useful – to the scene itself. When you get distracted, try shifting your focus to the person you're working with. Give them your complete attention and take the focus off yourself and the internal self-criticism that usually follows a distraction. Forgive yourself for being distracted immediately. It's normal and won't harm your performance as long as you can let it go. Your only job now is to continue with the scene, focusing on the person or objects in front of you, not on yourself as the actor. Think about it like this: when we experience pain in real life, if we shift our focus to something else, the pain is relieved. When I train at the gym, I focus on my breathing, and that helps me push through another rep. I focus on the strength of my legs rather than the pain. Similarly, when a child cuts their knee, giving them a sweetie miraculously eases the pain. When distractions arise and you start cursing yourself, for, let's face it, the inevitable – firstly let go of the inner critic and shift your focus to the present moment. Trust yourself, focus on your scene partner, and truly listen to them. Not just to their voice, but to everything they do. By doing so, you drain the distraction of its energy, reducing its effect on you. Silence the annoying voice of judgement, silence the fear, silence the inner critic so that you can let go and flow. I understand that this is not an easy task, so in order to get better at this skill, I encourage all acting students to practice mindfulness.

Mindfulness enhances our ability to live in the present moment as we become more aware of our bodies, thoughts, focus, and feelings on a day-to-day basis. Presence is a central goal for any actor during performance. The actor's job is to listen intensely, with all their senses, to deliver an organic and truthful performance. Actors must learn to stay focused whilst allowing unwanted thoughts (distractions) to leave their minds as quickly as they arise. I suggest practising mindfulness in your daily life. Take moments to connect with yourself and observe how you're feeling and what you're thinking. You can do this whilst walking in nature, sitting down at home, or anywhere else. Mindfulness is being fully present and engaged in the present moment without judgement or distraction. Distractions may momentarily derail us, but it is our ability to trust ourselves and our capabilities that allows us to move past them with ease. The more we practice mindfulness the better equipped we are at noticing our thoughts and letting them go.

An actor who is untrained in mindfulness has a tougher job staying focused than one who is skilled in this area. An untrained mind may start to wander further, causing stronger distraction and increased mistakes. Missed reactions and forgotten lines lead to frustration, and before we know it, we find ourselves "inside our heads" (a phrase often used by struggling actors trying to regain presence). We have ultimately made the distraction worse; the external distraction has caused an internal distraction, and the noise becomes unbearable. We gradually start to give power to the negative spiralling thoughts and consequently start to feel like a failure. In a short space of time (but what feels like an eternity) the mind starts to go blank whilst the body fills with unease, fear, and tension. More mistakes follow; the actor is no longer in the moment and free but is merely reciting lines. This leads to feelings of frustration, upset and fear. However, an individual who is practised in mindfulness is much better equipped to remove unwanted thoughts before they take hold and regulate their emotions so that they can return to the present promptly resuming the scene. In fact, no one would even notice the brief distraction.

Mindfulness is a powerful tool that can help you stay focused in the scene and manage any nerves that arise. It's safe to say that all actors will experience nerves throughout their career, although they may ease over time. Nerves trigger a fight or flight response that affects our working memory, leading to forgotten thoughts and lines. Therefore, it is crucial for actors to practice staying calm under pressure by utilising their breath when anxiety or stress creeps in. Breathwork has become increasingly popular as a daily practice for many people. It can help unlock blockages, change emotions, and manage stress. Our breath is directly linked to our emotions. By consciously changing the way we breathe, we can change our internal energy and emotions. This shift in the central nervous system signals to the brain that we are calm, and in turn, the brain will inform the body to relax. The brain and body are intrinsically interlinked, and gaining control over one allows us to control the other. Once we have a relaxed body, we have a relaxed mind. A relaxed mind means that we are the ones in control and we can direct our focus on where it needs to be. If you're interested in learning more about breathwork, I recommend reading *The Wim Hof Method* by Wim Hof.

Mindfulness can be practised in many different ways, such as keeping a morning journal, practising daily gratitude, going for walks and connecting to nature, practising breathwork, or attending yoga classes. The goal is to create an awareness of ourselves so that we feel connected to ourselves. Most people have forgotten to check in with themselves, their thoughts run unconsciously and so do their behaviours. The result means they compromise their emotions. Emotions are responsible for putting us into action. They ultimately decide what we do next. To manage our emotions means to manage our lives. Mindfulness brings our attention and awareness back to our body, our thoughts, and to the present moment. In time we start to become masters of ourselves and create an understanding of when nerves or tension start to creep into our body. With this knowledge we can use tools to gain control over our body and mind so that we can calm down and regain control of the situation. Mindfulness is a wonderful way to reduce anxiety and stress and can be one of the most powerful tools for an actor to master for both their career and their personal life.

Actors often find themselves in high states of anxiety which leave them feeling straight-jacketed and stuck. An actor's focus and energy may dissipate as overwhelming feelings of uncertainty creep in. We put pressure on auditions, fear not having work, worry about finances, and we feel sad when we don't get a role. These challenges can lead to negative and judgemental thoughts, comparisons, and blaming ourselves or others. Underneath the surface, anxiety can linger. It's easy for someone to say, "stop worrying, stop comparing, live joyfully, and calm the f**k down", but I understand firsthand how challenging it can be. The uncertainty and unpredictability of the industry can create frustration and anxiety, which often leads to stagnation and inaction. Who is motivated when they feel low?

Acting requires a strong backbone and an ability to find enjoyment in its unstable yet exciting nature. We cannot get wrapped up in overthinking or negative self-talk, but this often seems so easy to do. We must, if we are to stay in this industry, accept the industry as it is and accept ourselves as we are, not worse than we are. In this industry, it's common to not know when the next paycheck will come in or when the next job will come along. You may go months without auditions. It's crucial to accept this reality and learn to self-soothe and manage your emotions effectively. Ultimately, we must become masters of our emotions and our own best friends. The key is to become more present, where we cannot dwell on the past or worry about the future. When our minds are consumed by negative thoughts from the past, we can spiral into a state of depression. Constantly dwelling on failed auditions, forgotten lines, and missed opportunities hinders our progress. On the other hand, focusing too much on the future can lead to anxiety. The instability and uncertainty in this profession can trigger anxiety even in the most grounded and mindful actors. Recognise when this happens and don't bury it. Masking problems with quick serotonin fixes such as alcohol, food, or other distractions only hinders anxiety instead of helping it. Your body and mind are crying out for help, so do not deny this for yourself. Learn to listen so that you can rationalise your thoughts. Put pen to paper and get everything on your mind written down. Writing down your thoughts and concerns often alleviates many worries, but for those that remain, try to find solutions. If you're worried about your finances, what plan can you put in place to solve this? What jobs work well alongside acting? If you're worried about never getting a job again, are you catastrophising? Catastrophising occurs when we imagine the worst-case outcome in a scenario, which is usually unlikely. We must also change our perspective and we can only do this once we have alleviated the stress in the body by calming the mind. Remember, every experience is a learning curve, and you will get better at your craft and approach to the work every day. Be kind to yourself, learn from mistakes, and when negative self-talk arises, remind yourself that you are learning, and will *always* be learning.

If you have spiralling negative thoughts playing on a loop, ask yourself if what you're thinking is true. Most of the time, the "facts" we tell ourselves have no truth at all. We base these "facts" on past experiences that caused pain, particularly instances of rejection and disappointment. Setting ourselves up for failure inhibits hope, faith, and optimism, which are all essential for a happy actor. Therefore, we must challenge our thinking and consider alternative possibilities. How can you look at this situation in a way that empowers you? What action can you take to improve your feelings? Let go of what you cannot control and focus on what you can so that you can regain your focus and regain your motivation. If you weren't selected for a part because of a certain look, it is beyond your control and is not a reflection of your talent. However, if you didn't get the part because you didn't prepare enough, you can learn from this and then let it go. Beating yourself up is only warranted if you fail to learn. Choose to focus on growth and not stories of failure.

As an actor, it is important to discern what is within your control and what is not. Anything beyond your control should be released, or else you'll be trapped in a cycle of torture for the rest of your career. Work on understanding your fears by journaling or talking to a friend. Once you've uncovered your worrisome thoughts, rationalise your fears and create an action plan. It's best to do this from a state of calmness, which can be achieved through becoming present (mindfulness) and interrupting your breathing patterns (breathwork and exercise). Practising mindfulness daily allows us to master our emotions and our happiness, making us better prepared for what the world of acting throws at us.

TASK

1. Practice mindfulness daily. You can do this in many ways, such as going for walks, doing a body scan, practicing breathwork, or attending yoga.

2. Stay aware of your surroundings, focus on what you see in detail and the things that you hear and keep your senses active.

3. Try to focus fully on conversations without getting distracted.

4. Set an alarm when working or reading to maintain focus without getting sidetracked. Start with shorter periods such as twenty minutes and then gradually increase the time.

5. Try to remain present in daily activities like brushing your teeth or having a shower.

6. Journal whenever you need to.

2. Meditation

Meditation is a useful mindfulness tool for everyone, regardless of whether they are an actor. It allows us to detach from the stresses and spiralling thoughts of life. In meditation, the aim is to clear the mind of any thoughts, observing them as they arise and then letting them go. Meditation brings clarity, silence, and peace. Through meditation, we enhance self-awareness and gain insight into our thoughts and body. Often, we are too busy to notice the many thoughts that are triggered throughout the day or the stress and tension that is held within the body. Negative thoughts and tensions, if left unnoticed, can be destructive. What we think and how we feel in our body affects our emotions and emotions lead to action or a lack thereof. By mastering our thoughts and becoming aware of our bodies, we master our lives.

Meditation can take various forms and does not require a specific location. It can be done anywhere and at any time. Each individual will find their own meditation preferences, where they can access their inner world and inner calm. Guided meditations are available on YouTube; meditation classes or silent solo meditation are also other options. I personally love to attend a Yoga Nidra class or listen to a powerful guided YouTube meditation. I find that by practicing meditation I am able to slow down, not just physically but also mentally too. I can start to observe my thought processes and catch any limiting beliefs that may have a negative impact on my world. Actors experience more rejection, more silence, and more uncertainty. Constantly pitching for jobs and hearing the word "no" can make us feel uneasy and anxious. However, whilst we can accept these feelings when they arise, we do not have to dwell on them. We can use tools and techniques that can help us to change our state, reframe our thoughts, and ultimately raise our general happiness in life. For us to be able to use such techniques we must become self-aware.

Meditation provides us with a tool to become aware of our physiology (bodies) and the thoughts that are plaguing us. It gives us the space to become masters of regulating our thoughts and not ruminate on them, which can often lead to states of anxiety. We also learn how to calm the body down by focusing on the breath. With focus on the breath, we can adopt breathing patterns that activate our parasympathetic nervous system and calm us down. From this state, we can start to regain power over our thoughts. We are consciously developing the skill of being able to release unwanted thoughts through meditation. Consequently, when we practice this regularly, our neurological pathways become stronger, making it easier to release unwanted thoughts. Initially, meditation may feel uncomfortable or challenging, but the benefits are astronomical, both in our personal and professional lives.

Meditation gives us the space to observe our thoughts as we become more conscious of what we are thinking. Often, the unconscious cycling of negative thoughts can result in a lack of motivation, low mood, and general feeling of sadness. By reducing stress levels and enhancing focus and concentration, meditation has a positive impact on individuals. Individuals may experience something that triggers sadness and a stream of negative thoughts arise, but when you learn how to intercept these thoughts fast, they no longer consume you. In time, our ability to stay focused and ignore the thoughts that do not serve us becomes stronger. When you turn up for an audition, fearful thoughts may arise, such as "what if I mess up" or "what if I forget my lines". Often, we don't notice these thoughts; we only notice the emotional impact they have on our bodies – the nerves. Allowing negative thoughts to take hold can sabotage our best efforts in auditions or performances. Even if we do notice the thoughts, we must be able to release them and prevent self-sabotage, creating a better working environment within ourselves.

As an actor, you may encounter unwelcome thoughts whilst performing, often due to unforeseen distractions. For example, the director of photography (camera man) could be looking around and this might trigger thoughts like "what is he doing? Am I doing something wrong?" We must become skilled at releasing these thoughts so that we can focus on the present situation in our imaginary world. In theatre, there are often many distractions; a phone going off, a child crying, the irritating chewing noises heard from some woman in the front row who bought the entire range of M&S's biscuit selection. These distractions may trigger us and cause emotional reactions of frustration and annoyance, which diverts our focus away from the scene. We might start to curse and judge ourselves for not "being in it", then fears of "oh no, what if I forget my lines" come in, and we consequently focus on the fear, not on the present moment. Then, our emotions go awry. If this happens, the actor's performance may become compromised; therefore, it is essential the actor masters the art of catching this distraction early so that they can release it and promptly resume the scene. Mastering our thoughts and concentration is essential. If you struggle with concentration, focus, and negative self-talk, practice meditation. It has benefits that extend to both personal and professional aspects of life. Through meditation, we strengthen our ability to challenge negativity and stay present.

Recently, I observed an actress who was struggling to return to the present moment after forgetting her lines. After a great start, a minor interruption caused her to lose flow, and the scene started to deteriorate. Her sentences began to drop in tone, and her commitment and confidence were compromised. The initial mistake had ultimately cost her the rest of the scene. When I asked her what happened, she said she was consumed by thoughts of what went wrong and couldn't stop thinking about which lines were coming next for fear she would slip up again. I asked her how often she had experienced this, and she told me that she regularly struggles with making mistakes. Then, I suggested that she reconsider her perception of the situation. Perhaps what she considered a mistake wasn't the mistake. I told her that distractions will happen; it is human nature, and we must be compassionate to ourselves in those times so that we can release and let go. I then suggested that her only mistake was allowing the judgemental inner critic to compromise her performance and enjoyment of it. I encouraged her to start meditating as this practice would help her to focus. She mentioned her past struggles with meditation, unable to persist with the practice. I advised her to keep trying and explained that many people struggle at first, as it takes practice and determination to work past the brain's sabotaging thoughts of "this is a waste of time" and "I'm doing it wrong". I assured her that the main benefits of meditation come after continued practice, and as with every new skill, it's common to stumble at the first hurdle. This student did persist, and the positive impact of that persistence became evident in her future work.

Meditation may initially feel a little uncomfortable as we seldom allow ourselves to be alone and truly present. It can bring up thoughts we try and run away from, and it requires deliberate concentration and commitment, which can feel exhausting. To begin with, allocate ten to thirty minutes each day for the practice. If you don't have that much time, even five minutes is better than nothing. As you become more skilled, just two minutes at any point in the day will do. Meditation is a fundamental practice that helps individuals dealing with stress, anxiety, or depression. It is a significant tool for mental health problems.

In the past, I struggled with meditation as my mind was always on the go, so concentration didn't come easy to me. I also struggled to put my own mental health first and had a "bury it" attitude towards my problems. As you can imagine this attitude didn't serve me and neither did the excuse of "meditation is a waste of time". However, my research into the benefits of meditation could not be ignored, and the acting industry had started to make me pretty emotionally fatigued. I was burdened by the rejections, my self-esteem was on the floor, and this all coincided with that emotionally abusive relationship I was telling you about! I struggled with worrying about the next paycheck and fears about not getting roles. Riddled with anxiety, insomnia, and PTSD, I felt tense in everyday life and couldn't stay focused on the task at hand. In auditions, I was consumed by nerves and negative self-talk, which spilled over into my daily life. I never felt secure or stable, always feeling lost, stuck, and in limbo. I put my entire life on hold, afraid to make plans or book holidays in case a job came up. I put my mental health on hold convincing myself that I didn't have the time. Something needed to change. I felt that it was necessary – no, not necessary, but *essential* to persist.

Anxiety is a crucial, life-saving, organic defence system. It enables us to flee when in danger by directing blood to our limbs so we can immediately take flight. However, the dangers of the twenty-first century are very different to the threats this system was created for. Nowadays, threats come from societal expectations, fear of failure, and fear of judgement. These threats occur mostly within our own minds. The danger has changed, but the human response hasn't. Consequently, there are unwanted and unhelpful side effects. These side effects impact the body, including our breath, heart, vision, and central nervous system. Anxiety, once meant to protect us, can now be inhibiting, especially for individuals in high-stress jobs. The hormones released when we are anxious can immobilise us, making it difficult to think logically and redirecting our focus to the anxious feelings rather than calming the body and rationalising the thought that initiated the stress response. This can sabotage our performance and, most of all, our lives.

There are many forms of anxiety, from situational to more extreme forms such as PTSD. I unfortunately suffered with the latter. Meditation was without a doubt a tool that not only helped me to gain control over my life and work through my PTSD, but also helped me think logically in auditions. Meditation gave me the power to gain a greater level of self-awareness which allowed me to bring a sense of calm to what were previously stressful situations. My journey with meditation started quite early on in my career, but it took several years to become comfortable with it. It took time and patience. With persistence, though, much was gained. Now, I can often meditate for up to an hour, and I love it! Meditation empowers me to notice thoughts that I never knew existed, so I can accept them for what they are (just thoughts, not truths), challenge them, and swiftly return to the present moment, all in the space of a second or two. It helps me to become a more patient and understanding person as I become more patient and understanding of myself. It helps me to create an inner calm in a world filled with lots of external noise. It helps me slow down and learn about myself more deeply. I notice a significant difference in my mood and ability to stay present and regulate my emotions when I meditate. However, I must admit that even though I see such incredible benefits, I don't meditate daily and often blame time restraints, which is of course simply not true. We will all have habitual excuses that we use, and time is often one of mine. There will always be reasons not to do something, but it is essential to prioritise what truly matters. If I don't give myself time to meditate, I sacrifice my peace, my mindset, and ultimately, my life – which in turn affects all the people I love. Therefore, it becomes imperative that I hold myself accountable and dedicate time to this practice, not just for my own well-being but for those who I love.

Meditation has also helped me massively with auditions. I used to hate auditions, as I was often overtaken by nerves and self-doubt, but now I'm much calmer. I have learnt how to use my breath to slow down my heart rate and shift my physiology in a way that supports me instead of working against me. Immediately before an audition, I focus on my breath so that I can then rationalise any unwanted thoughts by reminding myself of what

I want to gain from the experience: to enjoy the moment, be present, and share my creativity as a collaborator.

Ultimately, working on being present and able to regulate my emotions has been fundamental in making auditions a positive and successful experience. There have been other major influences, such as aligning my self-image with the person I want to be and not the person I have been and developing a skill of self-trust – don't worry, we will come to these subjects later. But for now, understand that self-awareness is the first stage to making any changes. We have to know what we need to change before we can change. Meditation and mindfulness is a step that I believe shouldn't be ignored. If we can be so self-aware that we can stop the negative thoughts before they take hold, we can stop the catastrophising, and we can interrupt the fear. We will be well-equipped to start managing our emotions and, consequently, our lives. It's time to start trusting yourself, owning yourself, and understanding yourself so that you can create a better relationship with you! Let's start to notice our bodies and the destructive thoughts that are navigating our lives. Let's start to interrupt the cycles and the unconscious behaviours that simply are not serving us. Let's start to challenge the self-negative talk so that in auditions and, more importantly, in life, we can be the person we want to be, show up in the way we want to show up and live to our true potential.

Try it for thirty days. Try to meditate every day and let me know what you experienced – no, seriously, get in touch! Our lives are often so fast-paced, and we are always on the go. Sometimes, life can just pass us by as we get caught up in its busyness. We stop prioritising our need for space and silence; we stop prioritising our need to self-serve so that we can serve others. Once you start meditating you will not only show up for yourself more but also for every person you love and every person you audition for. Practice the skill of focus and practice the skill of thought extraction so that you are a master of clearing your mind and staying present. You've got this!

TASK

1. Practice meditation every day for thirty days. Start small, say five minutes a day, and gradually increase the time by one minute per day.
2. Check out Yoga Nidra – if you are finding yourself distracted or have learnt a lot of information in a short space of time, this will allow you to relax and digest what you have learnt.
3. Release the judgement you have towards meditation and understand that it is normal to feel uncomfortable, like you're doing it wrong or not good at it. Persevere.
4. Research the benefits of meditation.
5. Notice the excuses.

3. Self-Trust

How do we fully trust ourselves not to mess up? First of all, of course, do all the necessary work on the script to ensure that you understand your role and character. Then comes the fun part. We must remind ourselves of how we have trusted ourselves in the past. We are not only competent but strong, powerful fucking people, and we must start to trust ourselves NOW! Are you constantly seeking approval and reassurance that everything is okay? Do you often seek guidance before taking action? In general, do you trust your own judgement, or do you constantly rely on others to tell you what you should be doing? Do you value others' opinions above your own? If you answered yes to all of these questions, then you may be experiencing low levels of self-trust. Trusting ourselves stems from an innate feeling of self-belief, where we trust that our instincts and impulses are correct. A lack of self-trust can be linked to feelings of a lack of autonomy and control in our lives.

You must start to realise just how incredibly powerful you are. We tell ourselves stories of why we can't do certain things, of why we are not capable, and we back these stories up with evidence from the past, our experiences. Usually, we cling onto the negative experiences because our brain is wired to look for the negative more than the positive. After all, these are the things that could save our lives, right? Haven't you noticed that you can easily recall the insults that have been thrown your way but perhaps struggle to remember compliments? It is normal for the brain to look for the negative/danger and we should not judge it for doing so. However, constantly clinging onto our failures/insults/insecurities and not fully seeing everything that we have accomplished leaves one half of the story untold, and we need to re-tell that story!

We must accept that these stories are not accurate and challenge them. One client I was working with had an exam coming; I could sense it was making her anxious and she was very fearful of failing. When I pointed out that she has never failed any exam (this client was notorious for smashing her exams in the past; she is an extremely hard worker) she mentioned the time she failed her driving test and everyone was shocked.

I immediately replied, "Out of all of your wins, you choose to focus on that one 'failure'?".

To which she replied, "Yes, I am not sure why. I think it still affects me."

The perceived judgement from others for failing her driving test had created a trauma linked with the emotion of shame. Traumas, once locked in and not challenged, can debilitate us and cause unwanted states of anxiety and panic when triggered. Instead of focusing on the countless wins she had earned, this client focused on the one thing that she had failed to pass, which was making her emotionally vexed. Of course there can be ways to use pain to motivate and perhaps she was using this experience to motivate herself to revise, but in the meantime, it was sabotaging her peace and daily happiness. It was also making her question her capabilities and what was possible for her. Wouldn't it be better to trust yourself to do the work like you always had and walk into the exam with confidence in your ability? Wouldn't it be better to walk into that exam with a more peaceful state of mind where you can function effectively? If we can learn to self-trust whilst also keeping a high standard of ourselves, surely this is the winning combination? Do we really need to experience the pain? What else does the pain give us? Do you feel motivated when fearful? How much energy and time does it take? Do you feel happy in this emotion?

In my experience I am most powerful when I hold myself accountable to high standards but also have an uncompromising self-belief in my ability to succeed. I do not accept anything else. This way I can perform in an optimal state. So how did I get here? It wasn't easy and it takes time and perseverance, but it is so worth it! One of the ways I learnt to enhance my level of self-trust was to make a list of everything I had achieved and overcame in my life. That broken relationship, that poverty, that failure in English class, that win at sports day, that divorce, that childbirth, that acting class that you were so scared to take, that first home, that moving away from home, travelling alone, getting a degree, going to therapy, your first job. I mean absolutely everything. We often forget the challenges and hurdles that we have jumped over, and in doing so, we forget just how resilient, strong, and capable we are.

When I was suffering from PTSD everything felt impossible, and I felt like there was nothing I could do. I was in a pit of doom and intensely focused on how shit at everything I was and how it was all my fault. I focused on the shame attached to the abuse and on the guilt I felt towards myself for not loving myself more.

I blamed myself for choosing the wrong partner in the first place and for abandoning my friends and family. This resulted in a lack of self-trust. I wasn't using "failure" as a tool for growth, and I wasn't focusing on everything that I had overcome in the past and how resilient I was. I was focusing on everything I lacked and was not. Trust isn't just about making the right decisions. It's about knowing that you're capable of overcoming anything thrown your way. This way, no matter the outcome, you trust in your ability to face it. We must allow ourselves to fail, knowing that we have the ability to learn and grow from failure. We must rid ourselves of the need to be perfect. Perfection is not real and is rarely achieved. We must refrain from overly critical thoughts and from focusing on the perceived failures and inabilities that too often hold us back. Instead, we must create a new narrative. A narrative of wins and empowerment. We must strengthen our ability to self-trust by looking for evidence and examples of when we have done this. And I have a secret for you: all of us have done this. We are all alive and breathing right now. That in itself is a win. You have kept yourself alive. You have also dedicated time to reading this book and have kept going until now, which is more than what most people will do. That needs applauding and celebrating in itself because that tells me that you are taking ownership of your life, mindset, and future. Most people don't! So my task to you is a task of empowerment. It goes like this: write down your life story and write down everything that you have overcome. Bullet point your "failures" and reframe them as wins – what did you learn? Bullet point your successes. All of them. Do this NOW!

TASK

1. Write your life story.
2. Reframe your failures into learning experiences.
3. Bullet point your achievements and things you overcame.

The next thing to do is to start listening to your own instinct and intuition and not to other people's. Try to make your own decisions and take control of your own life. Obviously, seek advice and help if you require other people's expertise but smaller decisions such as where to eat out or what to wear are decisions that need to come from you. What decisions are you not making that you can start making today? Do you really need advice on which shoes look better? Do you really need advice on what to cook for dinner? Do you really need to lean on that person, or can you figure it out for yourself? The more that you do this, the more self-trust you will acquire.

The last thing that I want to mention here is very important. If you want to have a strong sense of self-trust you must...

Do the things you say you are going to do. You must hold yourself accountable.

The more that you show up for yourself every day and hold yourself accountable to your actions, the more you will believe in yourself. If you tell yourself you will train five days a week, do it. If you tell yourself you're going to go on that date, do it. If you tell yourself you're going to read that book, guess what? You have to do it! Whatever it is, show up for yourself and do not break your own promises unless there is a very valid reason.

This leads me nicely to compassion and empathy. Accountability vs compassion. Sometimes we might not be able to show up. We might get sick, feel overworked, need to prioritise our family or mental health, or there may be an unexpected situation that needs resolving. In these moments, practice empathy and compassion towards yourself. We must develop the skills to trust ourselves to do the right thing. Once again, this means seeing the whole story. We must be aware of the story we tell ourselves and of the truth. What are you not seeing? Are you being lazy, or are you extremely fatigued? Are you making excuses, or are you actually suffering from an illness? You must raise your levels of accountability whilst also being mindful that other factors in life affect us, and sometimes, compassion and understanding towards ourselves are required. A coach can help you achieve a greater level of awareness, as we often do not see our excuses so clearly.

Self-trust is something that can be acquired, and once you have done so, the impossible can feel possible. You feel empowered to take on the world and live out your wildest dreams. Yes, it will take time and patience, but the result will be an innate feeling of unlimited power. Surely that is something worth fighting for?

TASK

1. Practice accountability and do the things you say you're going to do.
2. Practice self-compassion.
3. Get a coach if you are struggling with either of these tasks.

4. Nerves, Self-Belief, and Courage

At this point, you should feel fairly confident that you have all the tools you need to deliver a well-rounded, thoroughly researched, and extremely present performance. The lights come on, the cameras start to roll, and people are watching. You're ready. Until suddenly, you're not. Your heart races, fear sets in, and things start to get a little hazy. People are watching – no, wait, people are *staring*, *judging*. If you're in an audition, you cling to your script; it's your safety blanket, right? If you're on set or onstage, you start to panic. You can't remember your first line. *Why can't you remember your first line?* You tell yourself to calm down, to focus. You tell yourself to concentrate. But when emotions are high, it's hard. It's exactly at this point that something has the potential to go "wrong". We can, if we allow it, experience an emotional hijacking. We freeze, unable to think straight, unable to function properly. So, how do we combat this? Let's delve further into some key strategies you can integrate into your daily life to help manage nerves. This is a very broad area, and there's no one simple and easy remedy. For some of you, nerves may always be present, but that's not necessarily a bad thing.

I, for one, struggled with nerves very badly early on in my career, and it was a journey to find ways to eradicate these or utilise them more effectively. I still experience nerves, but what I don't experience is a negative judgement towards them. I don't see them as bad, and I don't focus on them, so ultimately, I do not give them power. I have worked on my self-belief and made drastic paradigm shifts over the years. This means the nerves I once had now feel like an excited flutter; they are still there, but I love them. As mentioned a few times in this book, one of the most important things you can do is thoroughly prepare with the script. Belief and confidence come from within, and if you haven't put in the work, it will only breed doubt and trigger anxiety. The key message here is to do the necessary work to make you feel as prepared and safe as possible.

Nerves can also be channelled into the performance, especially if our character is experiencing a heightened emotion filled with energy. The nervous energy we feel can be transferred to the character's nervous energy by exploring the internal conflict they face. What's simmering beneath the surface of the character? What is the subtext? Is there a part of them that is upset, fearful, or excited? Nerves are essentially a build-up of energy, and if we can redirect this energy into something that aligns with the character, we can make better use out of it. This approach works best when there is an underlying emotional tension; it's not suitable for portraying a calmer state. I also advise you to use this technique with caution. Whilst it can yield good results, it can also be detrimental if used excessively or where inappropriate. It may lead to a performance that is excessively heightened or that becomes self-indulgent, filled with emotional energy but not much else.

Where is your focus? When you're nervous, your attention and energy tend to be directed inward, toward the nerves and fear. You become consumed by these emotions, seemingly unable to control them, and fear gains power over you. What if we shift that focus? Instead of focusing on fear, focus on hope and love. I often advise my students to carry something in their pocket that reminds them of how far they've come and why they started acting in the first place. For me, I love telling stories, and acting almost feels like meditation to me. It's a way to express myself and dive into my imagination. It allows me to experience intense emotions without owning them as mine. It's a detachment from my life and an adoption of someone else's, which brings me so much excitement and joy because I am obsessed with people and how our lives differ. It's also for that little girl who never thought it was possible for her to be an actor. The girl with the red hair and glasses who grew up poor but always had big dreams. Shift your focus to hope, love, and your ultimate goal, and utilise that to create your fight and drive. Once you feel energised and not fearful, it's time to accept that whatever happens happens, and there's nothing wrong with that. Let go and be present.

So take the time to explore your own personal "why". Why do you want to be an actor? Many actors forget why they do what they do. Instead, they put auditions, roles, or jobs on a pedestal, which leads to nervousness and anxiety. Matthew Mcconaughey puts it perfectly in his book *Green Lights* when he states that we need to **"become less impressed and more involved."** We must remember that we do this job because we love it. Often, we place too much pressure on a single audition, losing sight of how to enjoy the process. By shifting our focus away from the end result and what the casting director or director wants, we can enjoy the process and have fun. We can walk into every audition and performance knowing that we're serving ourselves and our love for performing. We can encapsulate the freedom, spontaneity, and incredible energy that we feel whenever we perform because we're not riddled with fears of not getting the part. We can shake off any fears of not being good enough, understanding that we're not there to serve the observers, but rather to serve ourselves. We must remember our "why". Why do you act? What does it give you? Does it make you feel alive? Do you love telling stories? Does it allow you to escape? By focusing on our why, we can approach performances with an elevated level of commitment, knowing that acting is a choice driven by our passion for the craft.

We must direct our focus also to listening. Listen to the people in the audition room carefully; listen to your scene partner, put your focus on them. Shifting your focus to them will distract you and keep you in the present moment. Fear cannot exist when we are truly present. Remember to breathe and prioritise relaxation. When you notice the nerves creeping in, focus on your breath. Sometimes, when performing, we forget to breathe, and the breath is the gateway to clear thinking. When stressed or nervous, we tend to breathe quickly or hold our breath, both of which reduce oxygen supply to the brain. Oxygen fuels our brains, so depriving it of oxygen impairs our ability to think straight. As already mentioned in this book, Yoga, breathwork, and meditation are excellent practices for becoming more aware of your breath and the benefits of slowing it down. Taking control of your breath nourishes your body and mind, providing the fuel they need to function. Remember, when you're nervous, breathe deeply and slowly. Changing your breath will ultimately change your physiology, which is essential for shifting your state. The body and brain are interlinked, so gaining power over the mind requires gaining control over the body. If the body feels calm, so does the mind.

Accept the nerves and face them head-on. When nerves initially arise, we might try to deny them. Unfortunately, this approach doesn't always work and can even amplify our nervousness. Have you heard the phrase "what you resist persists"? In my experience, there is a lot of truth in this statement. I remember a theatre performance I starred in that had numerous monologues in it. As nerves started to creep in, instead of letting them take hold, I looked out at the audience and just sat in silence for a moment. I thought to myself, *I am in control, the audience will wait for me.* In that moment, I realised the audience were in the palm of my hand, I was the one in control, not them, and that they were all on my side. This simple reframing of "I have the control" made me feel so empowered. I looked fear straight in the eye and it smiled back at me. I breathed into the audience, and when I felt ready, I delivered my monologue. Owning, accepting, and then looking fear head-on was liberating. I realised, in that moment, I wasn't scared anymore and all the work that I had done on my mindset had paid off.

This brings me nicely onto my next point: have the courage to fail. Failure is actually a positive thing that I encourage in most of my classes. I reiterate to all my students that the rehearsal and the classroom are the best places to fail, and we should forgive ourselves and even welcome failure. We shouldn't be afraid of it; we should embrace it. We've been taught that failure is bad, and we're well aware of the judgement we face when we fail. From school tests gone wrong to failed relationships, failure is never seen as positive. But how do we grow if we don't fail? How do we learn? How do we become more resilient? Failure gives us the opportunity to try new things and see what works and what doesn't. Many of my students tend to play it safe, constrained in their performances, scared to look the fool. When I encourage them to fail, they attempt new things in their craft. They become courageous because fear no longer holds them back. With new-found freedom and exploration, they make discoveries that offer valuable insights into improving their work.

Failure is also essential for emotional growth. I've witnessed students running out of the room in tears because they missed an emotional connection within the script and couldn't handle it. Some have left the class disheartened after a "failed" performance, forgetting their lines, or letting their nerves get the best of them. However, those who persevered after these very temporary setbacks always came back stronger. Such moments are often followed by a revelation, and the actors return with increased confidence, energy, and determination to succeed. They realise that failure didn't defeat them or their drive; it merely caused a temporary setback, a hurdle they had to jump. And once they were over that hurdle, they came back stronger. I recall being punched in the face as a kid. They mistook me for someone else, and we ended up in a fight. It was scary as hell, but the end result was that I didn't fear confrontation anymore. I realised a bit of a scrap really wasn't that scary. We often fear the unknown so much, but it's precisely those new experiences that empower us to soar and transform. With each new experience, we have the ability to learn and grow.

There will be times when we "fail" in high-stake situations like auditions or on set. In these moments, you have a choice: you can let your supposed failure hold you back, obsessing over negative thoughts and causing internal distress. Or you can bounce back, learn from it, and become stronger. When we accept failures, something unique happens within us – we start to lose fear. The worst has been upon us, and guess what? It didn't kill us; it wasn't that bad. Forgotten lines, freezes, and missed opportunities can either hinder our future, or serve as valuable learning experiences. We must be fearless in this industry. That, I can assure you of. Celebrate failures, as every failure brings you one step closer to success as long as you learn from it. Change your outlook, and your perspective will change. A shift in perspective is key to everything. With a new perspective, failures become learning obstacles – you didn't fail; you encountered a learning obstacle – and an opportunity for immense growth.

Practice makes perfect. I'll keep this point short and sweet, as it doesn't really need much explaining. Prioritise your practice and work on combating nerves. Face challenges by simulating experiences that trigger your nerves. Attend acting classes regularly, film yourself at home, and perform in front of others. By confronting these challenges, we become stronger in our craft. Practice makes everything appear more familiar, and we tend not to fear the familiar. Practising will boost your confidence and self-belief as you become more comfortable performing in front of others. Take on short films, seize as many opportunities on set as possible, and if you're just starting out, consider being a supporting artist for a whilst. Stay committed to your craft.

Now, let's talk about boosting your confidence. There are many ways to improve our confidence, and one of them is to uncover any conscious or unconscious beliefs that may be holding us back. We must do the inner work and identify anything that conflicts with our desires. How can we enjoy the process or be successful when something deep inside of us is running in conflict? Many of us hold beliefs that don't serve us, and the goal is to uncover and challenge them. Personally, I had an unconscious belief that people like me would never succeed, that I was an imposter who would eventually get found out. This belief stemmed from my experiences growing up, where I felt like the odd one out in every Drama class. It took me time to realise that my own limiting beliefs were generating my nerves and holding me back. I didn't believe I was worthy of success or that I could win because I didn't believe people like me won. What absolute BS!

It's crucial to become aware of any limiting beliefs that may be holding you back. You'll recognise them when you catch yourself saying sentences like "I can't do that", "that's not me", "I'm not good at that", "I can't get it", "I don't pick up things quick", or "I'm not a natural". Another indication of limiting beliefs is experiencing feelings of doubt, imposter syndrome, fear, discouragement, procrastination, and anxiety. It's your duty to unearth any beliefs that don't serve you, as a healthy mindset is paramount to your success.

Last, but most importantly, remember to enjoy the process. You chose this career because you love to act, remember that. Transform your nervous energy into excitement and possibility. Embrace collaboration and approach auditions with a passion for your craft and a willingness to learn without expecting a particular outcome. Enjoy going to auditions. If you don't enjoy them, start to, because they will constantly be a part of your career. Being an actor requires sacrificing a lot – we miss weddings, holidays, and birthdays. You will have to prioritise auditions above all else, and making a lot of sacrifices is necessary if you wish to be successful in this industry. If you don't enjoy it, there's no point in staying.

Serve yourself instead of trying to please others. Walk into the audition room, set, or classroom with the intention of having fun, and if you don't, seriously consider leaving the industry altogether. For someone who truly wants to be an actor, that statement should scare the pants off of you and should force you to enjoy the process. Make a promise to yourself that you will collaborate with the person in front of you – whether it's the casting director, fellow actors, or the director. Make a commitment to yourself to have a good time and trust in your expertise. Don't focus on what others think of you; it's beyond your control. Remember, you can't possibly know what someone else is thinking. Listen, be yourself, stay responsive, and work towards your objectives. I assure you, you can't go too wrong, and if you do fail, it's another learning hurdle that will help you next time. Well done!

One last tip is to use visualisation. Imagine yourself walking into the room and as the best version of yourself. Visualise smashing the audition or performance and owning the space. Vividly imagine how it feels. The next chapter will provide further guidance on how visualisation can help you.

KEY TIPS

1. Do the work.
2. Use nerves to your advantage when possible.
3. Remember your why and to serve yourself.
4. Don't suppress nerves but embrace nerves as excitement and focus on the love you have for your craft.
5. Practice your craft in front of others – practice feeling the nerves.
6. Remember to breathe.
7. Embrace failure as a learning opportunity.
8. Have fun.

5. Visualisation

Who do you want to be? Are your behaviours aligned with the vision you have for yourself? It's time to imagine what that new life looks like. We must have a clear understanding of our desires and the person we want to be. When we visualise, we allow our brains to recognise the things that we want to achieve with clarity, creating a specific destination. Without a destination in mind, we are lost.

Visualisation empowers us to become the inventors of our own lives. Every creation starts with an idea, so in order to manifest something new in our lives, we must have a clear idea of what we want to create. Consider how visualisation can impact different aspects of your life, such as family, work, home life, health, and self-image. How do you want others to see you? What behaviours would you like to embody? What vision do you have for your future? What house do you want to live in? How do you want to behave? In order to make changes in our lives and create a new future, we must understand where we wish to be.

TASK

1. What is your vision for the future?
2. Write it down in a paragraph with specific details.
3. Envision your ideal average day.
4. Identify the behaviours you want to embody.
5. Describe the person you aspire to be, someone uninhibited and fearless in pursuing their goals.

Once you have a clear idea of where you want to be, consider the impact it will have on your life. What is your reason? Without a strong "why" you will never fully commit to making any changes. Change is imperative to create a new life, but often people only change when they experience deep, incomprehensible pain. What is your pain, right now? Why do you need to change? What impact will this new life have for you and those around you? Be specific. How will it affect your finances, relationships, and sense of purpose? How will it impact the lives of others? Break down the reasons why you want what you want to truly understand what is at stake for you.

When I was younger, I thought I wanted to be rich. I thought that the reason I wanted to be an actor (other than loving the craft) was to become so wealthy I could buy myself and my family a nice home – one that we could call our own. As I got older, I realised that riches aren't guaranteed in the acting profession and that my "why" encompassed something much bigger than that. My "why" has changed over the years. In the past, I wanted money, acceptance, validation, and significance, but now I desire something different, something I think I've always desired deep down. I'm at a point where I feel comfortable in my own skin and financially secure, I have my own home, I can afford nice holidays, and I love the work that I do. Yet, I still yearn for more success in acting. Why? Here is my "why" broken down:

What Is My WHY?

I want to be a successful actor.

WHY?

So I can tell meaningful stories that inspire and entertain people.

WHY does that matter?

Because entertainment is crucial as it gives people an escape and instils hope.

Why is that important for you?

Because when I was a kid living in poverty, that's all I had – an escape through dreams of a better life. Films helped me do this.

Why does that matter to YOU?

Because I want others to feel that they can dream big and have hope. I want them to believe that they can manifest any life they desire, no matter who they are or where they have come from. I want people to know that they are not alone, that others like them have achieved the improbable, and I want them to feel inspired and motivated by that.

Why?

Because if a poor girl from Chesterfield can make it, anyone can!

WHY do you care about that?

Because I have experienced the suffocating constraints of poverty and the shame that it often brings. The hand-me-downs, the free school meals, the Netto shopping, the struggle to pay rent, the struggle to eat. I know what it's like to have big dreams but massive doubts because you believe your past dictates your future, and I empathise with every single person out there who has ever believed that they do not deserve what they want. I want to help people be free from that, from their limiting beliefs and from their internal struggles of self-loathing. I want to share the knowledge I have about mindset and prove that it is possible to be a happy actor and a successful one.

WHY?

Because with freedom, anything becomes possible. People can become whoever they want to be and live their life to their true potential. With freedom, individuals seize the opportunity to make the most of their one and only life. I want everyone to feel free and like they have a choice to do what they want. I want everyone to live with more peace, with more self-love, self-trust, and feel happier on a day-to-day basis. I know that as I become more successful in my acting career I will attain a status and credibility that will enable me to help more people and speak to more people about the things that are not serving them and what they can do that will.

My "why" isn't solely about myself now; it's about changing the world that we live in. It's about encouraging and inspiring, motivating and stimulating. It's about making a positive change in someone's life by proving that anything is possible if you really want it.

TASK

1. Figure out what your "why" is. Why do you want to be an actor?

2. If it's for acceptance and recognition, perhaps you need a more fulfilling "why". Your "why" should come from within you, not external validation, or you may end up disappointed.

3. Consider the impact of this new life. How will you feel? How will your life change?

Once you have considered the above, we can start the visualisation process. Visualisation can take place anytime, anywhere, and it doesn't need to be a long process. The important part is that the visualisation is clear, specific and that strong feelings are felt in the process. Remember emotions inspire motivation and drive people into action. Close your eyes, lie down, and envision the future you desire. How do you walk? Talk? Dress? How does it feel to now be living in that reality? What do other people say about you? What does your home look like? Your family? What does your average day look like? How do you now feel? Remember, attaching emotions to our visualisation will encourage us to take inspired action so that we move towards this goal. Whilst some people believe that visualisation alone will create change, I disagree. It is my belief that visualisation is just one part of the process, and the real results come from you taking action. The same thing applies to positive thinking and affirmations. You can tell yourself over and over again that you will wake up more toned, but without action, you will stay looking the exact same way you always have. Visualisation creates a clear end goal in our minds that we can work backwards from. It encourages thinking big because in our imaginations, anything is possible. Visualisation fosters focus, energy, and emotional drive towards what we want, motivating us to take action and allowing us to become more aware of the things that can help us along the way.

Motivation is the catalyst for action. When we feel motivated, we go to the gym, email casting directors, and work on improving our technique and mindset. Motivation drives action and taking action is what drives success. We must start to embody the person we want to be and start living the life we envision right now. Consider whether your actions align with your visualisations or if they are conflicting. If you want to feel beautiful in your body, are you conscious about what you eat and working out? If your goal is to get that first television credit are you actively emailing casting directors of soaps and television programmes in your area? Start to visualise the person you want to be and then visualise the actionable steps you need to do to get yourself there. Once you have done that, visualise yourself achieving the goal. This should give you the momentum to drive that action through. I remind you to add positive feelings to the visualisation. This is the most important part. You must feel excited about getting to where you want to be because this is what will drive you to take massive amounts of action.

TASK

1. Practice visualisation every day.
2. Visualise your success, the steps you need to take to get there and the person you want to become.
3. Determine actionable steps you can take today to progress towards your desired future.

Visualisation is a powerful tool that can greatly assist with auditions and overall goals. Footballers often visualise taking penalties over and over again because the same neurological pathways light up and strengthen during visualisation in the same way they would if they were actually taking the penalty. The brain cannot differentiate between a clear emotionally driven visualisation and the real action taking place. Concluding that we are more likely to do well in a given situation just by visualising it. We can use this technique towards our auditions and performances to enhance our success and ability to stay calm under pressure. Imagine the scenario in great detail, imagine what happens, how you perform, and how calm you feel. Visualise it going the best it could go and attach an emotion of pride and success to it and then see how this affects your actual performance.

Visualisation also creates a sense of familiarity of what is about to happen. This familiarity makes us less fearful of the audition/performance, as it is no longer the unknown. The brain likes certainty and familiarity helps to build upon that. We usually perform better in any setting when we know what to expect. If we are able to visualise the setting and the environment clearly, we can encourage a sense of familiarity when we perform. I often find that researching the casting director/director/theatre space/set or venue can really help with acquiring the specifics to create a more accurate visualisation. The most important part in the visualisation is to make sure that you visualise performing to the best of your ability, step inside your body and see it from your own eyes and not as an observer. Always remember to attach strong feelings such as calmness during the performance and joy and pride once you have achieved the success that you want. Visualisation gives us an arena to prime ourselves for success and rid ourselves of anxiety or fear. It enhances self-belief and motivation because if we can see it, we can believe it.

6. Fear

The entertainment industry can test our emotions daily. It's not a normal job nine-to-five. With high stakes come high emotions, and fear can often debilitate us. It's okay to feel vulnerable during auditions, performances, and in our daily lives. When we feel vulnerable, it often stems from fear. But if we accept the fear rather than trying to deny it or suppress it, we may just find that it isn't so bad after all. Accepting what we are feeling gives us permission to acknowledge and address it. We should never feel guilty about feeling the way that we do. Judgemental thoughts on feelings are never useful and only inspire more negative thought cycles. Remember, what you resist persists. Fear is a huge obstacle for actors – it comes in many forms: fear of rejection, fear of getting it wrong, fear of not getting a job, fear of losing an agent, fear of not being liked or accepted, the list goes on.

Fear affects us in various ways, both as actors and as humans. Fear makes us anxious, causes panic, accelerates our heart rate, and makes us feel out of control. Fear is so powerful it can discourage us when, in that moment, we need the opposite – we need to feel safe. Think about the situations where fear often arises: auditions, performances, first dates, rejections, interviews, public speaking – these are only a few examples of where you may have experienced the frustrating side effects of fear. Fear puts us into a mindset of lack, causing us to focus on what we don't have and what could go wrong rather than what is possible. It makes us risk-averse, closed off, and withdrawn. Fear makes us hesitant, causing us to stop and retreat. Think about it, when you experience gut wrenching nerves or anxiety do you ever feel motivated and inspired to take action? Or do you spend most of your time and energy ruminating over everything that could go wrong, why it will go wrong for you and make excuses not to follow through? Actors who frequently experience the debilitation of fear without implementing strategies to combat it are ultimately headed for disaster.

Actors are subject to many potential fearful situations. I remember one task in Drama School that terrified me: a one-minute stand-up comedy performance. It was only one minute, but still, I found the thought of this utterly horrifying. I felt vulnerable, exposed, and totally out of my comfort zone. The day of the performance loomed, and my whole body shook with nervousness. I felt sick. I wasn't a comedian, and I definitely did not find myself funny. I saw comedy scripts as my enemy, though, ironically, it's a genre I now work a lot in (remember your opinion of what you are capable of is the only thing stopping you from stepping into your greatness)! My fear stemmed from who I believed I was and what I thought I lacked or was incapable of. There was an internal conflict between the person I was trying to be, a comedian, and who I innately believed I was, a fraud, and this frightened the hell out of me. When our self-image doesn't align with the person we are trying to be, imposter syndrome starts to take hold. I was so fearful of the "guaranteed" judgement I was sure to receive from others and that I would be humiliated. My ego at this point was BIG, and looking back now I realise it was a mask for the deeper insecurities that burned within me.

The day of the stand-up came. Nerves overwhelmed me but shockingly the actual performance didn't go too bad; it actually went fine. I didn't freeze, and more importantly I didn't cry (I genuinely believed that I might), but the anxiety I felt prior to it made me doubt my entire commitment to being an actor. It was weeks of pure hell. Afterwards I sat in my seat proud of my achievement but also annoyed that I had allowed fear to ruin my experience. I was so focused on the fear, on the judgement and of not being good enough, that I lost sight of the fun I could have had and the growth that could have occurred. With a positive attitude that was focused on my personal growth and not other people's expectations, I could have leaned into it wholeheartedly and embraced the challenge but instead I recoiled and found the whole experience disheartening. This unfortunately became my experience of most of my auditions in my first few years out of Drama School. I hated them. I experienced massive amounts of fear and panic prior and massive amounts of disappointment after. Why? Because…

- I didn't understand how to manage my fear or my emotions.
- I was focused on the judgement from others and not my own personal journey of growth.
- I hadn't worked on my limiting beliefs (that I wasn't good enough / I didn't belong there). Instead, I tried to deny them.

- I hadn't aligned my self-image to the person I wanted to be or the person I had become. I was still that ugly ginger geek from that council estate with no prospects.
- I didn't know how to reframe my thoughts so that I felt empowered. Instead they consumed me.
- I wasn't aware of the stories I was telling myself or of the "truths" that were holding me back.
- I was too insecure.
- I forgot to have fun.
- I put every other person on a pedestal except for myself.

And all of these things combined resulted in FEAR. The later chapters in this book will focus on many of these areas in more depth and, if you resonate with my story, then I suggest you read them whilst taking notes.

Some Things to Remember:

1. Fear is not the enemy; your reaction to the perceived threat is the enemy. It is your job to master emotional regulation so you are optimally conditioned for success.
2. Other people's opinions of you matter less than your own opinion of you because ultimately the action YOU take affects your life.
3. Your limiting beliefs will always hold you back if ignored.
4. Your self-image must align with the person you want to be, and you must get clear on who that person is and what they look/behave like. Use the visualisation exercise.
5. Reframing thoughts is central to reframing your perspective. A better outlook leads to better results.
6. The stories you are telling yourself are rarely true.

7. Accepting and becoming aware of our insecurities and fears is the first step to working through them.
8. Judging our emotions will never help our situation.
9. That failure is learning.
10. If in doubt – have fun.

7. Fear of the Future

The acting industry is fickle and unpredictable. Jobs come and go quickly, and competition is steep. An actor may find themselves without work for a long period of time, leading to doubts, judgements, ridicule, and anxiety – understandably so. With no knowledge of when the next paycheck or role will come, an actor must build a life that can adapt to the unpredictable and interchangeable nature of the industry. This means pursuing jobs that they don't want but that offer flexibility. They may pursue temporary jobs and not a career because they believe they cannot commit to a career. This often leaves actors feeling stuck, as if they aren't achieving anything in their lives.

Consequently, anxiety rises, and the fear response is activated. When the one thing that we are putting everything into deals us regular hands of "no's", we start to doubt our ability. People need to feel validated in their careers; they need to feel like they are moving forward and significant. When they feel like their finances are stuck, their momentum has plateaued, and their prospects are low anxiety becomes high. The next audition consequently becomes a high-stake event because it could mean the difference between feeling happy and secure or feeling miserable and insecure. However, this fear and anxiety can show itself in the audition room, causing the casting director to recoil. The casting team can sense the nerves and desperation, and this causes them to feel anxious about placing their trust in you. You must remember the casting directors' status and reputation is at stake with every actor they hire. They need to know you can do the job and do the job well. A grounded actor at peace with themselves and the process is more hireable than a desperate actor living on the edge.

So how do we get grounded? How do we rid ourselves of the overwhelming fear when we don't know what the future holds? We cannot keep placing our happiness in the hands of something so unpredictable; we must take the power back. Actors must learn to listen to their fears and then come up with solutions to ease them. They need to address their insecurities instead of suppressing or denying them. If they are in a job that makes them miserable, they must find a way to support their career whilst feeling more fulfilled day-to-day. They must confront the tough questions that they may be scared to face. What can I do to release the fear? What do I need? More money? More security? A job on the side that I enjoy? What is within my control that I can change to reduce my anxiety and make me a happy, content actor? Whatever the overriding fear may be, actors must face it head-on and take action to change anything that is not working for them. By doing so, they can prolong their time in the industry and become happy actors, not just surviving ones.

Actors must use their initiative; they must be creative and think outside the box. During my time as an actor, I have also been worked as a waitress, a PA, a teacher, a writer, a producer, a support worker, a photographer, a receptionist, a voice-over artist, a presenter, a role player, a life coach, a casting director, and, of course, experienced unemployment. There are many jobs out there that can provide you with a source of income alongside acting whilst making you feel fulfilled, and that is the key. Most actors don't have regular work, so if you become one of the lucky few who do, congratulations. But my advice would be to find a job on the side that you enjoy, something you can do whilst building your professional credits. I know actors who have found fulfilling jobs that support their acting career in coding, personal training, assistant directing, therapy and counselling, nutrition, property, sales, and music. The scope is endless. The only thing holding an actor back from believing they can achieve wealth and prosperity in this field is their own mindset.

During my time as an actor, I have bought my own house, my own car, and I am self-sufficient. I do not struggle financially, and as you are aware, I have not had any financial support from anyone since before I left home. The path to financial stability as an actor is not like the regular nine-to-five worker, and that can make an actor feel like it's more challenging; in some ways, it is. Like any self-employed individual, an actor must find their own way, figure it out for themselves, and create a happiness strategy, not just a survival strategy. This means implementing action and making a plan. If you want to reduce fear or anxiety in your life, then you must take the power back and create a long-term plan of action that directly tackles your current fears. Only then can you create a career that isn't filled with resentment, spite, jealousy, and anxiety, but one that is filled with opportunity, passion, growth, and success. Too many actors focus on how to make a temporary living rather than how to create a lifelong solution. We must problem-solve the situation and not let the situation be a continuous problem for you! You could be auditioning for decades with no sense of progress. If you want to sustain a long-lasting happy career, you must make a plan to support this.

TASK

1. What are your current fears? Make a list. It could be wealth, a feeling of "not doing enough", a feeling of being stuck. Get clear on the things that are within your control that are making you feel rubbish.

In order to come up with solutions it is best that we get ourselves into a better state. A calmer one where logical thinking can be activated. We can change our state by using tools that will have a positive impact on our central nervous system and mood. There are many practices that I have found useful in reducing anxiety on a daily basis, including yoga, breathwork, exercise, walks and hikes, journaling, daily gratitude, healthy eating (reducing refined sugar and coffee and raising omega-three intake), motivational speeches, and music. It is important that you find the ones that work for you. We must also befriend fear, intentionally allowing it in and getting used to it when it rears its head. We must be comfortable with taking risks if we are to ever move ourselves forward. Risks are necessary to growth, so this means stepping out of our comfort zone on a regular basis.

Do that skydive you've always wanted to do. Ask that person out. Go to a dance class that you've been too scared to turn up to alone. Try stand-up comedy if you want. Whatever embracing fear means for you, do it. As I'm writing this section of the book, I'm doing a bungee jump tomorrow over Salford Quays. Am I bricking it? Yes! I'm absolutely terrified of heights! But I'm doing it anyway. Why? Because I will not let fear debilitate me or stop me from winning ever again. I have to experience real fear to put everything else into perspective. I have to test myself to see what I'm capable of, and with every new thing that I achieve and overcome, I feel stronger, more resilient, more self-trusting, and less fearful. I have found it useful for me, and I encourage you to try it. Do that thing that scares you. I dare you.

My last piece of advice is to detach yourself from any outcome or expectation when it comes to auditions. Fear can also arise from anxiety about what could be, about a desired future. See every opportunity and experience as nothing more than a moment in time for you to enjoy and learn from. It's an opportunity to showcase your talent, meet industry people, make new contacts, share your passion, and grow. Remove any form of expectation and detach yourself from a desired outcome. This way, you can enjoy the present moment and focus on it, knowing that you have nothing to lose and everything to gain.

KEY TIPS

1. Embrace failure and lean into it. Know that failure = learning, so it can't be that bad, right?
2. Listen to the fear and control what you can control by putting a long-term plan in place. What do you need to do to stop the anxiety? If you need more money, how can you get it? We must be conscious about making a plan otherwise the fear will keep raising its head until we give it an answer.
3. Regulate yourself with short-term practices that affect your central nervous system.
4. Become a master of handling fear by experiencing it often and stretching yourself.
5. Detach yourself from outcomes.

8. Silence

Have you ever looked at the letters within the word silent? They are the same letters that are within the word listen. I am a firm believer that in the silence, we hear more. As actors, we are trained to be incredible listeners (if trained well). We listen to the other actor, to our surroundings, and also to our internal responses – our instincts. To be a good actor, I believe we must be good listeners, and to practice the art of listening, we need silence.

To be intuitive, to understand ourselves, our thoughts, and our feelings, we must also give way to silence and make it an active component in our everyday lives. We must create space away from the hustle and bustle so that we can tune in to what our body and mind are trying to communicate to us. I used to shy away from silence, always on the go, always thinking, always on the move, always distracted. I liked being busy, keeping my mind active, and avoiding my thoughts – they were not often nice to me, so why would I want to listen to them? I didn't like spending time with my thoughts, I didn't like what they said, and the silence made me uncomfortable. I had spent years suppressing and hiding from my deepest insecurities but of course this never served me. There are many reasons why we may shy away from spending time with ourselves, but for me, it was due to initial feelings of discomfort and a desire to escape the thoughts I didn't want to face. If I bury my concerns and worries, they disappear, right? NO!

We live in a world filled with distractions, and we have become dependent on them, seeing them as the normal way of living. However, distractions are only temporary fixes for internal voids. Internal voids and anxieties can create blockages that manifest in unhelpful emotions. If you truly want to understand yourself and find peace, you must take time away to be with yourself. This time offers us moments of reflection, compassion, and understanding and allows us to consider how we can cultivate peace and balance in our lives. We must be proactive and receptive, re-evaluating where we are and where we want to be. It's crazy when you think about it – the amount of time we give to others, whether in work, friendships, or family, and the amount of time we actually set aside for ourselves. And I don't mean when we are being active, playing games, or watching TV. I mean *real* time with yourself. Taking yourself out on a date, going for a walk, allowing yourself to be fully present for a moment with yourself, journaling, working out, meditating. It doesn't have to be for long periods; a few minutes a day with yourself will make a difference.

Prioritising time for yourself is one of the best things that you can do. I spoke to a client I was coaching and asked if she ever spent her spare time alone with herself. "Yes, I bake. I make crafts," she replied.

"Sorry," I replied. "What I mean is, do you ever spend time going for walks, meditating, sitting with yourself in places where you can be with your true self?" When I said these words, there was silence. I explained the importance of silence and suggested she incorporate it into her own schedule, even for just ten minutes a day.

Her reaction said it all, "I need to be silent for ten minutes? What should I do? What should I think?" She was horrified at the thought. Sound familiar?

Maybe it resonates, maybe it doesn't. The shock for her was that she was so against it, as if I had asked her to go and spend ten minutes with her worst enemy or do something she absolutely detested. Why do we shy away from silence? From listening to ourselves? What are we hiding from? What are we scared to address? Sometimes ignorance is bliss, but then what happens? How does suppressing and denying manifest? Well, it manifests as internal blockages, unsavoury emotions, a lack of motivation or vision for the future, and unhealthy relationships. To create a healthy life, we must create a healthy relationship with ourselves and communicate better with ourselves. This means doing the uncomfortable work of finding our insecurities and the things we haven't dealt with and working through them.

Eventually, this client did start to include silent time in her everyday life. She set her own pace, one that she felt comfortable with, starting with just one minute a day of being with herself. She gradually increased this time by one minute per day until she reached ten minutes. Whilst admittedly she said this was highly uncomfortable to begin with, she did start to reap the benefits. Moments of self-awareness arose, and she became more in tune with her own desires instead of meeting others' expectations. She felt more present, more prioritised, and more at peace with herself. She gained a deeper understanding of herself, her insecurities, and her emotions. She was even able to express her insecurities to me, which she said made her feel like "a huge weight was lifted", as she was no longer hiding from them. Voicing them out loud also meant that the shame attached to them dissipated and she could welcome self-compassion into her life, understanding that these insecurities were created from a past trauma and to protect her. Self-awareness allowed her to take charge of her emotions, thoughts, and feelings – the ultimate source of power.

If you don't like being silent, you are not alone. Our modern-day brain, with all our contemporary woes and stresses, will try to sabotage our efforts to give ourselves this silent time because it feels that there's so much more we could and SHOULD be doing. We prioritise work, others, social norms, and social standards over our own need for clarity, insight, and self-reflection. Silent alone time will feel uncomfortable at first, and your mind may bombard you with thoughts like, "what's the point?", "this is a waste of time", and "there are so many other important things you could be doing". Allow those thoughts to wash over you and have faith that this time is necessary for your mental health, productivity, and self-care. When you prioritise yourself, and feel your own needs are being met, you increase your capacity to give and serve others.

The acting industry can often be a lonely place, whether on tour, location, set, or public transport to auditions. We are constantly with ourselves, and this allows for moments where we can really enjoy our own company if we choose to spend it that way. The more comfortable we become when we are silent and alone, the more comfortable we feel with others and in situations where we need to remain grounded and calm, such as auditions or performances. We start to appreciate our own company, like who we are, and, when this happens, we stop people-pleasing and feelings of inadequacy disappear. When you prioritise and appreciate time with yourself, your entire energy and belief system change. You enjoy being with yourself, and you believe you are a good and worthy person, so why wouldn't others want to work with you? This demeanour shines through not only in your day-to-day life, but in your interactions with acting professionals. You appear more grounded, connected, and present.

As an actor, there are many moments of silence throughout our career when things seem to come to a halt. It's important that we embrace those moments and find peace and calm in them, rather than fretting about the next role or job. Fretting is not useful – remember to emotionally regulate and then strategise a plan for your anxiety and then enjoy those moments of calm! Easier said than done, I know, but we must try to create the space we need during those times to prepare for what lies ahead. The life of an actor is full of ups and downs, highs and lows. If we never allow ourselves to step off the train, we will ultimately burn out. Our job is exciting, but it also brings a lot of internal stress due to nerves, expectations, and its unpredictability. It's not a normal nine-to-five; we are expected to be constantly on the ball, collaborating, and remaining flexible. We work a lot, juggling a hundred jobs to make ends meet whilst continuously adapting our lives in accordance with the demands of our acting career.

Things change at the drop of a hat – auditions come up, roles are won and lost – and you need to be ready. To avoid a burnout, we must interrupt the fast-paced nature of our work and invite silence into our lives. By slowing down and embracing silence, we can reap the benefits of a calm and peaceful mind. It may feel a little weird at first, but even just ten minutes a day in silence will do you a world of good. Prioritise your need for space and give yourself the gift of silence. If you miss a day or a week, don't judge yourself. Be compassionate and start again. As you practise, you'll start to recognise when you need these moments of silence and listen to that inner voice.

TASK

1. Allow yourself to embrace silence. This could be through an active practice like going for a walk or simply sitting in silence.
2. During the silence, pay attention to your thoughts. What are they telling you? What do you need to address?

9. Negative self-talk and limiting beliefs

Here's the truth: as humans, we tend to have more negative, self-critical, pessimistic, and fearful thoughts than positive ones. Why? Because the brain defaults to worrying about the future. It's always on the lookout for danger to keep us safe. Negative thoughts account for 60–70 percent of our brain's activity. This survival mechanism is essential; it is much safer to mark something as a threat than safe. We are hardwired to look out for danger, and we see this in our everyday life. We learn to look before crossing a road, avoid touching electric fences or hot stoves, and plan our commutes to prevent being late for work and potentially getting fired. The danger may have changed what it looks like – the scary hungry animal has turned into your annoyingly naggy boss – but the danger is still there. Forward thinking and considering potential risks are essential for our survival, but sometimes we can obsess over the fear too much. So much so in fact that it prevents us from ever reaching our true potential and taking action.

Years ago, this survival instinct came into play when we were faced with real danger that could ultimately end our lives. In the twenty-first century, this survival instinct arises when we feel unsafe in a bit of a different way. We are bound by fears of judgement, ridicule, rejection, lack, discomfort, the unknown, embarrassment, social shame, wealth, and disrespect just to name a few. For actors, these fears often raise their heads during auditions and performances. The unfortunate reality is that when we need to appear calm and focused, we are often taken hostage by our emotions. Cortisol courses through our veins, our breath quickens and becomes more shallow, and we start to sweat. Unable to think clearly or function properly, we are unable to process feedback, take notes, or access our working memory. For actors, this is an absolute disaster.

If we are going to interrupt this cycle, we must understand its origins. The trigger is usually either the thoughts we have and/or the body's alarm signals. When triggered, our body reacts with an increased heart rate and heightened alertness. The trigger could be from anything, but you will know when it happens because you will feel it inside of your body. It's here that negative thought patterns can spiral and repeat over and over again as you start to feel more and more out of control in your body. Concerns and worries about what could go wrong are made worse by the drumming in our hearts. Our gut tells us something is or could go wrong, and we fall into the trap of catastrophising. Many of the thoughts we experience in this heightened state of alertness are not useful and are often very unlikely. Thoughts and the body's alarm signal can be stimulated and triggered by anything the senses can pick up. A smell linked to a time that you received some awful news or a song that was playing at a funeral. Some triggers we are aware of, others we are not.

It's important to remember that the body and mind work together. Once negative thoughts arise and spiral, the effect on the body is immediate and an emotional response created. Once an alarm signal goes off in the body it immediately prompts fearful thoughts as you start to feel out of control. These emotional responses are directly responsible for what happens next, as most humans react in accordance with their emotions, not logic. The sight of a boy who rejected you makes your heart race; you remember the pain and feel embarrassed, so you decide to walk the other way to avoid him. This pain can lead to anxiety and lingering thoughts of not being good enough throughout the day. Similarly, the smell of an ex may make you feel sad and resentful, which then manifests in blaming yourself and consequently feeling pessimistic about the future. Thoughts and the body's internal alarm system directly shape our feelings.

Negative thoughts about ourselves and our capabilities often arise from our limiting belief systems, which are shaped by negative experiences and low self-esteem. Such thoughts can lead to sadness and a lack of motivation. When a negative thought is triggered by a limiting belief, it elicits an unwelcome emotion and compromises our central nervous system. The central nervous system is the body's processing centre, responsible for collating information and coordinating activity throughout the entire body. Therefore, it's crucial to maintain its proper functioning. Negative thinking and self-limiting beliefs can have highly detrimental effects on both our body and mind. If our unconscious beliefs directly affect our thoughts, mood, and behaviour, it's an area nobody should ignore.

So why do negative thoughts hold power over us? Negative thoughts derive from our belief systems, which, despite not always having a positive impact on our lives, have developed as a safety mechanism to protect us from harm. Consider phrases such as "I can't do that", "I'm not good at that", or "I would do that but…". These phrases all inhibit an individual because they hold the belief that taking action will result in failure. Failure is associated with rejection, which translates to loss of love and acceptance, something we all deeply desire. Painful experiences therefore create unconscious scars that remind us to avoid any similar experiences where we might experience loss of love and, in doing so, inhibits our growth. We must, if we wish to grow, become increasingly aware of the negative thought cycles and deep-rooted limiting belief systems that continue to hold us back.

What we believe we can and cannot do significantly impacts the choices we make regarding our future. If we believe that the world is against us, it will affect every interaction we have and everything we do. We may avoid opportunities out of fear of failure or because we distrust others. Consequently, we refrain from putting ourselves out there because "what's the point? It won't work anyway" or "they will only judge you". These beliefs become the centre of our worldview, and we constantly seek evidence to reinforce them. We will focus on aspects of our lives that confirm our beliefs due to confirmation bias (a tendency to find comfort and confidence in validating our beliefs). You may observe friends and family members doing this all the time, stating a belief like "the rich don't care" and actively seeking evidence to support this belief. Such a belief views the rich as adversaries, which could sabotage any attempts to achieve financial gain.

So how are these beliefs formed and how do we change them? Essentially, a belief could have been formed at any time or place – an embarrassing situation, a parent's influence, or an insult someone said to you at school. The problem is beliefs can become so ingrained in us that we might not even know their origins or be consciously aware of them. Our beliefs are also incredibly fixed, which restricts our view of the world to only one side of the coin. Humans learn from past experiences, and once the lesson has been learnt, we store it as a belief to save time and energy – the brain simply cannot focus on too many things at once. We then do anything we can to reinforce that belief because humans crave certainty. However, these lessons can often be detrimental to our judgement as we mistakenly link present experiences to similar (but not identical) past ones, denying ourselves opportunities to learn, grow, and seize new possibilities.

The brain's ability to adapt and change as a result of past learning is often referred to as brain plasticity. This incredible mechanism that we hold within us teaches us to avoid danger or persist in achieving our goals. With every new experience, more information is stored in our memory bank of "truths", which ultimately shape and influence our future behaviours. We are the product of years and years of reprogramming, and each individual's programming is different and unique. This reprogramming of the brain is essential to our survival. However, due to the massive amounts of experiences and beliefs stored (many of which can be contradictory), sometimes this programming is inaccurate. As a result, we function like faulty machines, interpreting one situation in the same way as another and responding accordingly.

Consider this example: a year ago, you went up to someone and asked them out, and they rejected you and then laughed. Cruel, I know! As a result, your ego was badly damaged, and you experienced pain, rejection, and suffering. Six months later, the same thing happened again. Awful. Your brain stored these encounters as painful experiences and formed a belief to shield you from such pain from ever happening to you again: "don't ask someone out because you will get rejected". Then, you meet another person who you find attractive. You're flirting and there's evident chemistry. You want to ask for their number, but your brain has adapted, and you feel huge resistance that prevents you from taking any action. Your "intuition" and "gut" tell you it's not the right thing to do, or is it? This current situation and the past ones are different in so many ways (different person and time and different you), but your brain fails to recognise this and treats them as if they were the same. This learnt behaviour, born out of fear and a desire to avoid pain, may have saved you from rejection before, but it has undoubtedly inhibited you from getting a date with someone in the present moment.

So let's break it down. There was an incident that caused a negative emotion, which created a trauma, and that trauma led to a lesson intended to protect us from future pain. Useful, right? Most of the time, yes. However, occasionally, no. Some beliefs can hold us back. We can become overly cautious, engaging in avoidant behaviour and not facing our fears. This avoidant behaviour leads to inaction and lack of growth. Although this avoidance brings immediate anxiety relief, it strengthens the cycle of avoidance. So, how do we work through this? First of all, you need to become aware, and this is not always easy. Tracking thoughts and beliefs that you might not even know are there can be challenging. A good coach can be helpful in identifying your limiting beliefs quicker and holding you accountable for changing them. Limiting beliefs are so ingrained in us that without external eyes and ears, we may really struggle to locate them. With the help of a coach, I became aware of the negative beliefs

I didn't even know I had. I learnt that I held limiting self-beliefs about my social class, morality, romantic relationships, self-worth, self-trust, and self-love. Once I became aware of these beliefs, I was able to start working on them. If you cannot afford a coach, it's still possible to do it alone, but you must be unrelentingly persistent. You need to learn how to emotionally regulate, reflect, and listen to yourself and your responses. You must stay accountable, be flexible, and seek the truth, even if it challenges the narratives we tell ourselves. Uncovering traumas and limiting beliefs can be intense, challenging, and uncomfortable work, but it's paramount to your success. Once these beliefs are unearthed, you can reframe and dismantle them so that they no longer hinder your future growth.

In the grand scheme of things, what matters most are the implications of these beliefs – how they affect you now. Do they strengthen or immobilise you? For example, if a teacher once said we were not smart, it could have various implications. As the comment came from a teacher, we might respect their expertise and believe it to be true. We may start to feel embarrassed, unworthy, and insecure about our place in the world, questioning our acceptance by others. To protect ourselves from feeling the burden of this insecurity, we may adopt certain behaviours. We may label ourselves as "not smart", keeping us within our comfort zones. We keep ourselves out of harm's way and deny opportunities for growth and learning because what's the point? "I'm not good at it, and I don't want to be called out again. That was painful". This self-protection strategy denies us the chance to learn and grow, shielding us from the pain of judgement and failure.

On the other hand, we may take the opposite approach and become obsessed with validation and hard work. We believe that we need to work excessively hard because things don't come easily to us. This may result in perfectionism and a need to constantly seek praise from everyone else. However, this praise often only temporarily fills the void within ourselves. We constantly seek reassurance from others, unable to make decisions out of fear of getting it wrong, thinking "I'm not smart enough" and "others know more". This manifests as procrastination, lack of self-trust, and a lack of acceptance of our abilities.

So what do we need to do? We need to realise that the belief is not currently serving us and is inaccurate. What part of the story are we not seeing? What else could be true? We must find ways to validate and back up a better belief that will serve us. Old belief systems that are not serving us need updating and challenging.

When I was younger, I had bright red hair, a pale thin face, and big glasses. I was considered different, ugly, teased, and called names by many school kids. I held onto the belief that I was not beautiful and was different for all the wrong reasons for years; it actually followed me until my late twenties. I still carried the self-image of that bullied, ginger, geeky kid from school. I couldn't even close my eyes and imagine the woman I had become; all I could see was the past version of me. A belief of who I was and what I was capable of had been instilled. I struggled with my confidence growing up, I struggled with relationships, and I compared myself to others all the time. I never thought I would be desirable to anyone because deep within me, I still felt substandard, ugly. The effect this belief had on my self-worth and self-esteem caused inaction and greatly inhibited my growth until the belief was challenged and reframed into something that would serve me.

Another limiting belief I held onto was about my social status and what I thought I was capable of. I thought that being from a low-income family meant that I would never succeed in acting. I would always feel like an imposter. Why? Because acting is for the elite, and everyone who did it had money and came from a good family. I, on the other hand, grew up on a council estate and wore hand-me-downs from the kids on the next road. This belief was not serving me or helping me achieve my goal. Did the fact that my family had no money stop me from making amazing friends, doing the things I wanted to do, and becoming the person I am today? No, if anything, it contributed greatly to all of those things. It gave me more independence, more dedication, and much more resilience and tenacity. The point is, we must find what our limiting beliefs are so that we can challenge them and then change them to work with us and not against us. We change them by gathering evidence to support a better belief!

It is at this point that I would like to mention that pain can be a useful tool if used carefully. When we experience pain, anger and fear often come with it. Anger is incredibly useful for motivation; if you can navigate anger efficiently, you can acquire huge amounts of motivation and take action. Pain is a useful tool when navigated well, as humans will move away from pain quicker than they will move towards pleasure. We can use the pain we have felt to fuel us and motivate us, to prove people wrong, to succeed in spite of others' opinions, and to become the person we desire ourselves to be.

The shame I felt regarding my poverty and family's stature growing up meant that I did everything in my power to move away from being poor as an adult. It meant that I became self-sufficient and financially stable. However, it also meant that I had an unconscious limit of what I thought was possible for me. In one regard, it has fuelled me, but on the other, it has kept me from reaching my full potential. Until now.

Learning how to utilise pain effectively to achieve motivation is powerful, but we must also understand how that pain may cause insecurities and create certain beliefs that could interfere with our future progression and general well-being. For myself, I wanted to succeed to prove people wrong, to show them what I could be and what I could do. I unconsciously used the pain of poverty and judgement to fuel my work ethic. However, other people's judgement was not only my motivator, it was also my undoing. The pain of what others had thought of me in the past fuelled me yes, but also debilitated me. Every time the memory was replayed it was strengthened. Every time I saw myself as a victim, as unworthy, in my mind I lost power over myself and the doubts I held about what I was capable of would creep in. A constant search for validation made me focus on other people's opinions instead of my own. It also meant that I was unforgiving towards myself at times and relentless to the point of extreme fatigue and burnout.

Pain can be useful and remembering what you don't want can be motivating, but remember, pain can also cause insecurities, and self-harming behaviour may debilitate us. No success is worth an endless supply of self-torture. Reframe the past so you are not a victim; see your pain as your strengths and show the world what you are capable of. Searching for validation is an endless task you must validate yourself. Only then will you have a fire inside of you big enough to take on the world. You must remember both what you are moving away from and why, and what you are leaning into and why. Who do you want to be? Who do you need to become to win? How can you reframe the past to feel stronger? How can you destroy insecurities that are holding you back? What stories are you telling yourself that are simply outdated and not true? Humans change every day; you are not the person you think you are, and the reality is you can become anything you want to be as long as you have a vision for it. Challenge the negative self-talk, challenge the limiting beliefs that do not serve you, and challenge the stories that are not true. Once you have done this you must align your self-image with the person you are transforming into, the person who you want to become.

In order to do this, we need to get clear on what we want in general. What is your life's mission statement? Be specific. We must all have a plan for our lives. If you don't, you will get swept up in the busyness and demands of twenty-first-century living, and in the blink of an eye, you'll miss it. It is time to get your plan together so that you can figure out who you need to become to complete it.

TASK

1. What is your mission statement? Your goal for the future?
2. What stands in the way of you achieving this goal? Consider any thoughts, realisations, or beliefs that stand in the way of you achieving your goal.
3. What stories are not serving you? How can you reframe the past to make you strong? What are you not seeing?
4. Who do you need to become in order to win?

Negative self-talk is something that I am certain we are all guilty of at one point or another, both in our professional lives and our personal lives.

Do these phrases sound familiar?

- "That was really stupid."
- "Why did I say and do that?"
- "You're an idiot."
- "You can't achieve that."
- "That isn't possible for you."
- "What are you doing?"
- "You aren't good enough."
- "You aren't getting anywhere; you might as well just stop."
- "What's the point?"
- "This is taking too much time."
- "This isn't ever going to happen."
- "I'm not smart enough."

It is an unfortunate truth that at some point, some of these phrases have played over and over again in our minds. We, as humans, can be our own worst critic at times. When something doesn't go the way we expected and we have been impacted in a negative way, the unwelcome self-made critic will pop into our heads to repeat the things that we have done wrong. These thoughts are like a tape recorder on a constant loop, and we become haunted by our mistakes, what we should have done differently, and how stupid we are. These repetitive, habitual cycles of thoughts often make us feel unworthy, incompetent, and untrustworthy. When this cycle of negative self-talk occurs, the thoughts become amplified, stronger, and empowered. This can, if we allow it, result in a low mood. When we experience a low mood, our passion, commitment, and motivation decrease, and everything that we thought was possible seems harder, if not impossible, to obtain. That audition, that role, that possibility of making it all seems like a pipe dream. This lack of motivation results in a lack of energy and a lack of willingness to succeed and win. So how do we stop this clear derailment?

Imagine yourself as a train with a destination of where you want to be. You pick up speed and momentum in moments when you are feeling positive, motivated, and empowered. But then something happens that challenges those thoughts. A rejection from an audition, a performance that didn't go as planned, or feeling jealous of your friend's successes. These challenges lead to thoughts that change your perspective and attitude. You become discouraged, unmotivated, and start questioning why things aren't happening for you. This halt in momentum, energy, and vibration causes your train to stop.

However, it's important to remember that every train has stops along its journey. These are necessary for refuelling, recharging, and reflecting. We have a choice at these stops. We can either allow negative thoughts to consume us and potentially even end our journey, or we can continue on and utilise these stops to pick up valuable lessons and drop off harmful thoughts, emotions, and beliefs that discourage us.

If you have felt jealous or uneasy about another's success, that is a normal reaction, I imagine most people have felt this at some point and arguably continue to feel like this. I know that before I worked on my mindset, I too at times would feel like this; however, it doesn't mean we have to accept it. Perhaps it's time to do some inner work to explore what is being triggered within you and see how we can change our reaction so that it works for us and not against us. Perhaps it reveals that you are focusing too much on others instead of the only thing that matters and that you have control over, yourself. Perhaps you have a tendency to live in a lack mindset thinking that there is only a limited amount of success available? Perhaps you are feeling impatient, meaning that you are unhappy with your current situation. What is your learning? Find out and act on that. In the meantime reframe your perception so that it serves you. If others can succeed, so can you. If you've faced rejection and felt deeply hurt by a lost role, reframe the thought to focus on what you gained from the experience and see it as an opportunity to grow and to become more resilient.

If you feel impatient, stuck, or lost, it is important that before you try to think your way out of it you change your state so you feel more motivated and positive – solutions are harder to find in darkness so we must look for the light. When you feel energised, positive, and have a brighter outlook on life, everything seems possible; however, when we are clouded with darkness, negativity, and fear we feel hopeless and like everything is against us. To change our state we must change our physiology, breath, and body. You must find what works for you. We must move in a way that makes us feel powerful and breathe deeply. In these lower moments, go for a run or do some yoga or breathwork. Inspiring speeches and inspirational talks from a mentor or someone you admire can also be useful. Please refer to the chapter on positivity and motivation for more information on how to change your state and emotional regulation.

Once you feel more uplifted you can start to identify what is missing in your life and take action to address it. Are the thoughts you have even true? What part of the story are you not seeing? Are you focusing on what you lack and fear of the future or are you focusing on what you have achieved and what is possible? Use these stops in your journey to realign yourself, remind yourself of what you have accomplished, celebrate your successes, and stay focused on your destination. Use this time to make goals, plans for the future, and, most importantly, focus on yourself. Refrain from judging yourself; we all compare and feel stuck at times. The important thing is what we do in those moments. Do we allow them to swallow us up into a pit of darkness, envy, and resentment or do we use these moments to learn more about ourselves and what we want in life?

TASK

1. Consider any negative thoughts or beliefs you may have had recently about your acting or the acting industry. Identify a better, more useful thought or belief to have. Cross out the old belief and write a new belief that will help you achieve your goals. For example, if you wrote "Acting is hard", you may replace it with "Acting is a worthy challenge".

2. Reflect on your limiting beliefs. If you are struggling to answer this question, think about what makes you feel insecure, what triggers jealousy, and when you find yourself comparing yourself to others.

3. Consider if the opposite of your limiting beliefs is true. Spend time finding evidence to support the opposite belief. It may be challenging, as our brains tend to seek evidence that supports our existing beliefs.

For example:

Limiting belief: "I am not smart enough."

New belief: "I am smart in my own way."

Proof: "I am an excellent drawer and have high levels of emotional intelligence."

Always choose to believe something more empowering that will move you forward.

We cannot control what thoughts come to mind, but we can control which thoughts we give power to. It's crucial to be mindful of the thoughts we give the most energy to as increased energy results in increased power. Think of it like this: if I were to ask you to remember a time your partner or parent hurt you, you would likely remember it instantly because you've replayed that memory repeatedly. However, if I asked you to recall what you had for dinner two days ago, you might struggle to remember. The energy we give something grants it its power over us. If we repeatedly play the same scenario from a detrimental perspective over and over again in our minds, that will destroy our self-esteem. Notice what you are giving your attention to, what beliefs and thoughts are dominating your mind, and whether they are justified and helpful for your desired path.

Limiting beliefs often operate unconsciously and strengthen as we gather more evidence to support their truth, making it harder to dismantle them. When these beliefs take hold, we may feel down, unmotivated, and lose sight of our strengths, the future, and the things we have to be grateful for. Positive beliefs about ourselves can inspire, motivate, and drive us to take action. Conversely, limiting and negative beliefs can lead to stagnation, depression, and a constant feeling of being stuck. It's important to remind yourself that not all your beliefs are true. Just like how many people believed the world was flat or that bats were blind (they can actually see – yes, I was shocked, too), beliefs about ourselves should also be examined critically.

Beliefs are created from our past experiences, social norms, from labels that have been put on us, and from the opinions and views of others. They stem from past pain, learning, and the "mistakes" we've made, as well as the assumptions from others and ourselves. Beliefs become ingrained and habitual thoughts ensue. These ways of thinking occur unconsciously. For example, a client held a limiting belief that losing weight meant that they wouldn't be fun anymore and people wouldn't like them, so instead of sticking to a healthy eating plan they self-sabotaged consistently and unconsciously so that they didn't face rejection/judgement from others. The belief was formed by a flippant comment a friend of the client had made when she refused an alcoholic drink. The friend had said "don't be boring", and this comment embedded a belief that cost the client's own happiness. The belief was then backed up by any other evidence that they could find until challenged in our sessions. Once challenged and proved untrue, the client lost the weight and felt happier following her own goals and desires and not living her life according to the destructive views of others.

Whilst many things can contribute to forming beliefs, not just other people, it's worth recognising that as we change, expand, and grow every day, many of the beliefs we hold onto are outdated. We are not the same person we were when the belief was first formed, and spending our time and energy on inaccurate and unhelpful beliefs that no longer serve us is counterproductive. You have the power to become the person you want to be by simply choosing to think differently about yourself. You have the power to follow your own desires instead of giving power to the judgement of others. The only person who deserves power over your life is you.

At school, I was a smart kid, and always did well in exams. However, in one particular lesson, I was messing around, and the teacher said that I would need to listen because I would struggle in the next exam. She also mentioned that creative writing wasn't my strength, and that writing in general was a struggle for me because I was not grammatically strong. Looking back at this comment, it was unjustified. I was sixteen and had never had any problems in English exams before; I was a straight-A student. Yet, after that comment, I became overly concerned about the approaching exam. I doubted my abilities and what I was capable of due to this teacher's words. I came out with an E. I was a grade-A student, and I got an E in one exam because I allowed a teacher to instil a belief and an expectation of what was possible for me, and I chose to believe it. When I retook the exam, I didn't put in extra preparation or revise more, but I told myself that I was not going to let that teacher's comment affect me. I got a C, a much better grade, but still not in line with my other grades. In all other exams after this, I achieved A grades. Can you imagine what would have happened to me if this comment had been more generalised across all my studies?

What if the teacher had labelled me as slow and incapable in primary school? What if they had called a meeting with my parents to say I would struggle? What if this was then reiterated to me throughout school by my parents, who wanted the best for me so wanted to ensure I worked hard? What if my grades got better, but the feeling of unworthiness and not being good enough remained? What if the past labels echoed loudly in my mind for the rest of my life? What if my belief system had been compromised, leading me to frequently voice statements that reaffirmed these beliefs, such as "I tend to struggle when learning a new skill" and "I'm not naturally very smart". How would this manifest in my life? Perhaps I would be reluctant to try new things and learn. Perhaps I would be lacking in confidence and often feeling overwhelming anxiety, especially in academic settings. Maybe I wouldn't pursue my dreams or commit to anything due to fear of failure. Maybe I would never want to showcase my work just in case people thought it wasn't very good, so I hoarded my talents. What would the implications be for me and my future? What is the cost of the beliefs that you hold that do not serve you?

The power of one comment that we store as truth can have massive repercussions over our lives. How many opinions and beliefs do you hold about yourself right now that are harming your progression? How many are based on absolute truth? Realising that our assumptions can be wrong and that our beliefs are not based on absolute truth means we can channel our energy into creating new empowering beliefs. When we genuinely believe in our potential and that something is possible for us, we become inspired, motivated, and energised. This changes our approach to everything, and a world of opportunity opens up for us. We don't have to live and abide by a past-defined identity. There are no limits to what we can do and achieve. With every new day, we have the potential to become everything we desire. Some things may be more challenging than others, but without restrictive labels, they become attainable, and we can take the necessary actions to enforce them.

Take a closer look at the belief systems that no longer serve you. What negative limitations do you hold about yourself? Write a list. Examine what evidence there is to prove this. Is it truly an accurate representation of who you are? What self-imposed labels have stopped you from doing things? Building a strong and empowering belief system essentially means re-evaluating old beliefs and asking ourselves, "Is this belief really true?" If it isn't serving you, we must attempt to get rid of it. Be kind to yourself but honest. You must see things as they are, not as you think they are. Look for specific evidence to challenge your belief. Ask a friend to help if you can, then take action to reinforce the belief you want to have.

The next step is to start taking action to work towards your new belief. Look for things you can do now to back that belief up. For example, if you have a belief that says "I can't trust myself", look at when you did trust yourself and what you have accomplished and then start taking action to trust yourself more on a day-to-day basis. If you have a belief that says "I am not a good writer" but you want to write a book, then look for evidence to disprove this belief and work at creating the skills to be a writer. Sign up for a writing course or start writing for one hour a day. In time, your self-image will align with the action you're taking, and you'll start to see yourself as a writer, and a good one at that, because you're behaving like one and have developed the skills to become one.

If you have a belief that states "I am not a working actor", then actively start searching for jobs on a day-to-day basis, don't rely solely on your agent. Write and create your own work. Utilise social media. Think outside the box, email, and make connections on a daily basis. Remember, the reality of an actor is remaining consistent, developing a strong technique, networking, and job hunting, it is not just filming every day. Live the reality of an actor, the real life, not the glamorised one, and in time you will start to feel like a working actor. It's time to step up and become your own advocate, fighting for a more positive mental attitude toward yourself so you can achieve everything you ever wanted.

Remember, it's all about reaffirming and creating beliefs that serve you and dismantling the ones that don't. Years ago, I used to believe that good actors needed natural ability. This belief didn't serve me, as it meant I was constantly seeking for validation in my acting, and if people didn't say the words "natural talent", I was ultimately left disheartened. It also meant that when I first started coaching actors over a decade ago, I held a belief that didn't serve my students. Very quickly, though, I realised that anyone can be and do anything they desire, and that anyone (with a good work ethic and training) can become a talented actor.

When we lose our outdated negative belief systems, we change the way we think, and we free ourselves from limitations. We can create our future based on our desires, not our past. Whilst it's important to manage our expectations and make sure our goals are achievable, we must remember that our minds often gravitate toward problems rather than possibility, so always challenge yourself. By changing our perspective, our behaviour, and the actions we take, we can change our lives. When we become aware of our destructive thoughts, we can stop ourselves from catastrophising and procrastinating. Learn to be aware, to pause, to challenge those thoughts, and then create new belief systems that serve your well-being and help you reach your destination.

TASK

1. Remind yourself of your new beliefs daily and create affirmations to reinforce them.

    Affirmation examples:

- I am smart.
- I am talented.
- I create the life I want.
- I learn quickly.
- People respect me.
- I am worthy.
- I am valued.
- I am confident.
- I am committed.

Affirmations, when regularly spoken out loud, allow us to take ownership of our new identity and shape our behaviour. The impact of the words we use and how we describe ourselves is huge, so we need to start to take control of that now. It's time to notice how you talk about yourself to others. When you notice yourself saying something negative, STOP! This can be difficult at first, as we may be so accustomed to speaking negatively about ourselves that we don't even realise it. But by tuning into the things we say out loud about ourselves, we can start to understand our belief systems better. The negative self-talk we voice becomes self-made prophecies. What you think is possible for yourself is the only thing that matters, as all success stems from an openness to receive it. Eradicating limiting belief systems can take some time and requires conscious effort, but if from today you begin your journey of noticing the language you use, you're certainly one step closer to freedom. Many of my clients are shocked and upset when I repeat back to them some of the words they use to describe themselves during our sessions. They are astounded that they could be so cruel and lack so much compassion. Some of the things we say to ourselves we wouldn't dream of saying to our worst enemy, let alone our best friend. Your task now is to become your own best friend.

Being your best friend means understanding yourself, showing self-compassion, having your own back, and knowing that you deserve the life that you want. We enter this world alone and we leave it alone. At the end of the day, the only person we can truly rely on is ourselves, so we need to create the most resilient, motivated, energised, compassionate, and forgiving version of ourselves. Negative self-talk impacts how we approach the world, determining what we believe is possible or not. Remember, everything we do is a direct reflection of our thoughts. Thoughts are influenced by our core values and beliefs, which can either motivate us (when positive) or stagnate us (when negative). What we say about ourselves is a choice. Do you choose to be motivated or stagnated? Do you choose to hold yourself as a winner or a failure? A victim or a hero? Whilst it is important that we build specific affirmations that align with a desired self we must also be conscious about taking daily action to reinforce such affirmations. If you have the affirmation "I am worthy", you must become aware of your boundaries and your values and live in accordance with these things. If your affirmation is "I am smart", you might take action to learn new things or teach others what you know. If your affirmation is "I am beautiful", when you look in the mirror, you should try to see at least one thing that you find beautiful about yourself. Always consider how the person you want to be would behave. Words matter but actions matter more. It is our ability to live as the person we desire that will enforce the necessary changes to become that person.

10. Positivity and Motivation

Acting can be a challenging industry, and there will be times that you beat yourself up. Auditions and performances will likely go wrong at some point. You might forget a line, lose a job, and feel like the world is crumbling around you. But when this happens, you have two choices:

1. You can allow the feeling to swallow you up whole, changing your mood and energy for a lengthy period of time.

OR

2. You can implement a strategy to change your state and mood for the better, staying positive and becoming more resilient.

It is not your situation that causes long-term suffering. Yes, the situation impacts us and causes the initial discomfort, but it is our perspective and the actions that we take afterwards that are responsible for long-term suffering. If we can change our perspective on what is happening to us, we can change everything. So, how do we do this? How do we remain positive when faced with rejection and suffering?

1. **Know how to motivate yourself.** When you experience a setback, it can affect your state of mind, so you need to know how to regulate it. You can change state very easily if you know how. I do this in my client sessions all the time and they are often astounded at how quickly they are able to shift from one emotion to another. One quick tip is the use of memories that you hold dear. You can ground yourself with a memory alone. Thinking about a fond memory and

taking yourself back there can be a very powerful tool. You might also find motivation by watching an inspiring film at the cinema, listening to music, writing, or by doing something physical like dancing. What inspires you? Once you understand how to elevate yourself, it becomes much easier to change your perspective on things because your mood has shifted. Everything feels more possible when we are happier. Top tip: the breath signals to us the way we feel, so start by changing your physiology. Yoga, breathwork, and exercise are the easiest ways to do this. The body and breath change with our mood, as the brain and body are interlinked. Once you have achieved this you can start to motivate yourself with your mind. Visualisation can also be useful. You can visualise what happens if you don't change or stay in this low state. Pain can be a huge way for us to feel motivated towards taking action. I like to visualise both what happens if I don't change or get what I want and then what happens if I do.

2. **Remember why you do it.** Acting is tough, but it is also exciting, invigorating, and brings joy. Every day is different. You are one of the lucky few who gets to do what they love for a living, so don't beat yourself up for choosing to live the life of your dreams. When you fall, get back up fighting, and when you crumble, rebuild. Do not bully yourself, and do not greet yourself with disdain; be your own best friend. Write a list of why you want to be an actor and the positive things it brings to your life. Remember the LOVE!

3. **Support yourself with a job you enjoy and find rewarding on the side.** I mentioned this earlier in the book, but it really is important. If you don't enjoy what you do on a daily basis to support your acting career, then you'll become resentful towards acting. If you're at peace in the life that you're building and appreciate the other things that bring in money, you won't mind so much when you don't get an audition. You won't see it as "your way out" or "your escape"

because you enjoy the life you have now. You might believe that becoming a famous actor will make you happy, but the reality is this actually might not be true. Are you willing to sacrifice your immediate happiness on the prospect of future happiness? Or are you going to start now? Find another job, one that is fairly flexible, of course, that stimulates you and in which you can grow and feel financially stable if this is a concern for you.

4. **Set goals outside of acting and don't make acting "the be all and end all".** I have seen many actors fall into this trap and develop an unhealthy relationship with acting. It becomes almost like an obsession. The acting profession isn't one that we have lots of control over; ultimately, our success is often in the hands of other people, and we have to be okay with that. Yes, there are things we can control, there are also lots of other things that we cannot. Being obsessive is not a useful tool, especially when it negatively impacts your overall well-being and happiness. Remember that there are other areas of your life to focus on: romantic relationships, finances, spirituality, fitness, family, friends, career outside of acting, and education. What else do you want to achieve in these areas? To be truly happy and content, we must draw attention to all aspects of our life.

5. **Compare to empower yourself.** See others' success as a possibility of what can happen to you instead of dwelling on what hasn't happened. Don't see another's success as an excuse to bring yourself down; you don't need that, and it isn't helpful. Try to remain hopeful. It's happening for them, so it can happen for you too. Changing your perspective may take time, so accept that it won't happen overnight and be patient. Don't judge yourself for comparing or feeling negative initially. This is normal, and we have been programmed to do this. Remove the judgement so you can release and reframe.

6. **Be resourceful instead of resentful.** How can you benefit from the success of others? If someone is achieving the type of success you want, instead of being resentful, wouldn't it be more useful to ask them how they did it? Learn from their strategies to grow and improve yourself. It's better to approach the individual with kindness and warmth rather than resentment. Often, individuals who achieve success are met with hostility and resentment, so kindness and support would be welcomed. We must celebrate the success of others, knowing that there is more than enough success to go around.

7. **Remember everything you have achieved so far.** Make a list of all the things you have accomplished, from performing in front of an audience for the first time to filming on set in your first leading role. Don't hold onto past pain. It's easy to remember all the rubbish and things that made you feel low, but if we hold onto these things, we attract more of the same. Focus your energy where it serves you better. Remember the good memories and try to learn from and make peace with the painful ones.

8. **Take action.** You are in control of your own life. Take daily action to reach the place you deserve and need to be. Don't overthink it. Focus on the small things that make the big difference: email casting directors, network, create your own work, practice your technique, and act on any feedback you receive in classes. Work on accents, new skills, and challenge yourself constantly. It is only through action that we move forward. Some of my clients worry they are not doing enough. It is important to know what enough is for you. How many hours a day, a week? Be specific with time or any other quantifiable goal. One hour a day, or ten emails a day, it really doesn't matter, just use what works for you.

9. **Don't neglect your diet and your health.** Your happiness is massively dependent on the food that you eat and the exer-

cise you do. Since most of our serotonin is produced in the gut, we must be mindful of the impact of our food choices on our mood. Foods that spike cortisol levels (stress levels), like refined sugar, are obviously going to affect your mood negatively. Be aware that a spike in cortisol leads to a decrease in melatonin; the result is low mood, insomnia, and inability to digest food properly. An imbalance of omega-3 and omega-6 can also significantly affect your mood. I highly recommend reading the book *Why We Eat Too Much* by Dr Andrew Jenkinson, as it provides valuable insights into the role of food on our emotional well-being. Remember to move your body and to exercise. The effects of exercise are well known; it boosts our mood, improves sleep, and reduces anxiety. As an actor, your body is your instrument, so it's important not to neglect its health and strength. Remember, everything you feed your body feeds your mind. The body is our vessel, and we should work hard to keep our vessel free from pollutants and energised.

10. **Get lots of sleep and rest.** Downtime is important. A lack of sleep affects our mood negatively. Don't overlook your need for a good night's sleep. If you struggle with sleep, then create a sleep routine that works for you. A good strategy for a good night's sleep is essential. I have found meditation music, black out curtains, staying away from my phone one hour before bedtime, a morning walk, not eating two hours before bed, and chamomile tea all very useful solutions. Make sure to regulate your parasympathetic nervous system (this is the nervous system that activates a calmer state) by taking rest during the daytime. Yoga Nidra, mindfulness, meditation, and going for walks can all help with this. This will reduce stress and enable you to be more patient and ready to handle whatever challenges come your way.

11. Goal Setting and Achieving Clarity

What do you want to accomplish in the next month, three years, or five years? It's important to be specific. To get the life that we want, we need a strategy. Goals hold us accountable and prompt us to consider the necessary steps to reach our destination. In the acting industry, it's easy to sit back and just allow things to happen, especially if you have an agent. But this attitude is not one that will help you succeed. It is my belief that the most successful people don't just work hard, they use their time in the best way possible to get them where they want and need to be. They are efficient with their time and consider different routes to get to their destination. They think outside the box and take responsibility instead of blaming external factors. Whilst luck and timing do play a role in success, dwelling on them and attributing our lack of progress to them is a waste of time. Excuses do not serve us; they only provide an escape from taking action and hinder our progress. We must focus on the aspects within our control, such as networking and creating industry relationships, practising and developing a strong acting technique, strengthening our mindset, and creating our own work instead of waiting for the phone to ring.

What can you incorporate into your strategy to encourage success and growth in your business? What goals can you set that you have control over? Acting is a business, and you must view it in that way. What specific targets can you set for yourself? Can you dedicate an hour a week to networking with someone new via telephone, in person, or online? How about finding an agent? Can you dedicate more time watching things that inspire you? Can you learn how to write, direct, or produce to further your understanding of the industry and potentially open new doors? Can you spend time researching casting directors, getting to know local production companies, and finding out about local castings? How about accents? Can you grow your accents so that you feel confident performing in these? Do you want to get fit and regulate your bad eating habits so that you are healthier and happier? What belief systems or habits need changing? How can you use social media like LinkedIn? Identify what aspects are most useful for your journey. Most people will say they have tried everything but this is rarely true. What are you not seeing?

I encourage you to take the first step towards goal setting by coming up with a comprehensive list of actions you can take to attain the life you desire. From reaching out to people via email to writing your own film, I dare you to open your hearts and activate your imagination. Don't worry about the specifics for now, just start with defining what you want to accomplish. Once you have your goals in mind, you can determine the necessary steps to reach them.

TASK

1. What actions can you take that are within your control?
2. What are your goals for the next four weeks?
3. What are your goals for the next six months?
4. What are your goals for the next twelve months?

Once your goals are set, you need to remember why you have these goals and what it will mean for you. What difference will it make if you learn a new accent? What difference will it make if you go to the gym five times a week? How will it affect you physically, emotionally, and psychologically? Your "why" needs to be strong, as it provides the motivation and self-discipline needed to pursue your goals. Self-discipline can be challenging, especially for actors who often struggle with impatience. We want everything now, but the reality is that just doesn't happen for most actors. How can you cultivate more self-discipline? How can you take action even when we don't feel like it or haven't seen the results yet? Here are some top tips to enhance your self-discipline:

1. **Don't let yourself think your way out of something.** If you want to go to the gym or get up early, don't allow yourself to even consider not doing these things. Let your body move before your mind can stop you. Instead of contemplating excuses, take action.
2. **Create a compelling "why"!** Why is it important to you? Make it matter. Do you want to feel healthy or be around to watch your grandchildren get married? Which one is stronger?
3. **Identify belief systems that may contradict the actions you wish to take.** If you want success but believe it will lead to isolation and resentment from others, you might self-sabotage. If you want to have a hot body but believe sugary food is what makes you happy, you will not stick to the diet. If you want to make more connections and network but feel you are not a people person and people do not tend to like you, you will not go. What are the beliefs that are holding you back?
4. **Utilise your pain as a driving force to move away from what you no longer want.** Consider the consequences of not making a change. Understand that others cannot persuade you into something unless you truly desire it. If you want to lose ten pounds because your partner is doing it, this reason may not give you the strength to resist the triple chocolate Oreo muffin. However, if you want to lose ten pounds because you have a history of heart disease and obesity in the family and recently had a health scare, perhaps the next time you look at that muffin you'll think twice. People often change when the pain of remaining the same becomes unbearable. I changed massively after experiencing PTSD – I had to change; there was no other option. I couldn't continue living as I was.
5. **Take accountability.** It's easy to fall back into old routines and ways because they are so heavily ingrained into us. This often occurs when we are stressed or upset. Hold yourself

accountable, or even better, find someone to hold you accountable. At the same time understand that we cannot control the experiences that happen to us. We might get poorly or experience a loss. In these moments, be compassionate to yourself and give yourself time to heal.

6. **Make time in your diary.** I organise my diary with specific tasks for specific hours to help me stay on track. Instead of having one big to-do list, I set time aside for each item so I know that it's achievable. I even block out time for the gym because this means I will go. I set time aside for meditation, reading, writing, lunch, work, and pleasurable activities including me-time. Yes, me-time! Since I love my job, it's easy for me to lose track of time, so I must be conscious about how I use it.

7. **Encourage self-discipline in all areas of your life.** Like any skill, it needs practise and development. Something as simple as not hitting the snooze button causes a significant change for most people; it affects how you approach the day and shifts your perspective on waking up. When we snooze we are filled with resistance but when we turn the alarm off and shoot out of the bed with energy we are charged.

8. **Be careful not to become a pleasure seeker.** We can easily become addicted to pleasure because the world has made everything so easy for us. This has consequently made discomfort very unappealing. If you only pursue pleasure, why would you want to do anything else? To achieve what we want, we often must make unpleasant sacrifices, but in the end, this act of delayed gratification gives us the most pleasure and makes us feel fulfilled. Ensure that you don't become solely driven by instant pleasure or dopamine-seeking behaviours, as they can significantly impact your success.

9. **High intention low attachment.** Avoid becoming overly attached to the outcome and instead focus on enjoying the ride and being consistent. If you can try to find a way to enjoy ev-

ery audition and every email sent to a potential connection, you will do it more and the people on the receiving end will feel your enthusiasm. However, if all you focus on is the potential outcome you lose the enjoyment of getting there. You stop focusing on learning, growth, and fun and instead opt for people-pleasing, anxiety, and "getting it right". Change the intention to something fuelled with enthusiasm and motivation and people will feel it.

10. **Success takes time – usually.** Yes, occasionally people will get lucky; however, those who are committed and consistent tend to be the most successful. The reality in this fickle industry is that there will be highs and lows, and there will be busy times and quieter times. But if you take action and work hard towards your goal every day, then you are more likely to get there.

TASK

1. Hold yourself accountable or find a coach or friend who will do that with you.
2. Follow the steps above.

In the acting technique section of this book, we talked a lot about stake. What is at risk? What is there to gain? Consider this deeply when reviewing your goals. Each goal requires an unwavering commitment level of eleven out of ten. If your commitment level is anything less than that, you must look at the reason why. What is causing that blockage? Is it an attitude? A belief? Negative thinking? Lack of energy? Lack of time? What excuses are you holding onto? Yes, excuses. If you want to make new connections and email more but feel your commitment level is at a five out of ten due to lack of time, how can we put a strategy in place to ensure you have the time to prioritise this? Perhaps it means going to bed one hour earlier and waking up one hour earlier in the morning, perhaps cutting down on TV at night?

Every gain requires some sort of sacrifice, and it's crucial to be okay with that. Understand the gain and understand the sacrifice clearly and be honest with yourself – are you willing to make that sacrifice? If I get up one hour earlier, I get to write that show I have always dreamt of writing. The sacrifice is that I will need to go to bed earlier and miss watching *Come Dine With Me*. Is it a sacrifice worth taking? Most people don't consider the sacrifice and then become disheartened when they realise it's necessary. Prepare for resistance by understanding the sacrifices involved. Once you know your obstacles and areas of resistance, you can come up with a solution to counter that.

TASK

1. Reflect on your commitment level for each goal.
2. Consider the sacrifice you need to make and anticipate when resistance will arise. How will you cope with that?

We need to find a strong strategy to ensure we stick to our goals. How can we make these goals happen? Start with asking yourself a series of five questions, the first being *what?* What can help us to achieve our goal? What are some of the actions we can take? Can you hire an accent coach, take acting classes, join a gym, join a yoga class, learn to meditate, read more, or watch more film/television and theatre? There are many strategies you can employ to reach our desired destination. For instance, if our goal in the next four weeks is to learn an accent, we can consider purchasing an accent book or getting an accent coach. We can also utilise YouTube or learn from a friend. Immersing ourselves in the accent authentically can also be beneficial. You can also take a look at websites or other resources to help you make progress. Remember, nothing is impossible, even with limited finances; the key is to find a way.

The next question is *who?* Who can help you achieve your goal? I recently invested a lot of money in a coach to help me on the next stage of my journey, because I know that the pain of losing that money and not making it back will be unbearable for me, so I will succeed. I also believe that he has the right strategy to help me, because he has done the same thing I'm aiming to achieve and possesses the necessary resources for me to progress. Someone who has faced similar challenges can serve as our guide. If we need help with self-belief or overcoming self-worth issues, we should seek out individuals who have successfully done so and learn from their experiences.

How? How can we achieve it? Do we need to implement a schedule, get an accountability partner? What do we need to sacrifice in order to achieve the goal? How can we stay motivated? We need to commit 110 percent to our goals and recognise that we are solely responsible for our own success. Remind yourself daily of the goals, the reasons why they are important and the strategies you have in place to achieve them. If you are not prepared to go the distance, then there is absolutely no point. Growth isn't easy, and sacrifices will need to be made, but that is the whole point of delayed gratification.

Why? Always relate your goals back to your overarching desires and objectives identified in the visualisation exercise. You must remember your *why*. Why must you do this? What will change in your life if you make the changes today? Remember the power of visualisation and use it to understand the necessary steps for moving towards your desired life.

Where? Where are you now and where do you want to be? Get clear on the destination. With no destination you roam aimlessly. Have a clear path.

TASK

1. Consider the *what, who, how, why,* and *where* for each goal.

It's important to set achievable goals; otherwise, discouragement, loss of motivation, and decreased commitment levels may follow. Regularly check in with yourself and assess your progress. Personally, I find it helpful to dedicate every Monday to review my progress, identifying what actions are moving me towards my goals and the things that are not working and may need adjustment. It is important to be flexible with your approach and strategy. If things aren't working and you are losing momentum and commitment, look to others who have achieved what you want to achieve. How did they do it? Look at their strategy, immerse yourself in their story. Find inspiration from other success stories and utilise that to get excited. Whatever you do, keep going, keep motivated, and remain focused on your own journey. No one is like you, no one has lived your life; therefore, comparing yourself to others is pointless.

Everyone is on their own journey, you included. Compare yourself to your past self and celebrate the progress you have made, regardless of how big or small. Stay in your own lane and avoid comparing your success to others. If you feel yourself getting jealous, reframe that as excitement and potential success. When someone lands a role or has a big win, let it inspire you, as it proves that is possible and attainable for you. Reframe negative thoughts and change your perspective to work for you, not against you. Regular check-ins can help assess your happiness within the industry. It's okay to leave or take a break if you need to. Remember, your mental health and overall well-being should always be your number one priority.

12. Compassion to YOU

Be mindful of yourself and your mental health. Take the necessary steps to take care of it. This profession is unique because unlike most people, we are constantly interviewing for jobs, often facing rejection on a monthly, weekly, or even daily basis.

This constant cycle of rejections and job hunting can be mentally, emotionally, and physically exhausting. Our hopes are built up only to be shattered in the space of three days. Constant dopamine highs and lows result in actors feeling in a constant state of panic. It is crucial that we show compassion and kindness to ourselves, recognising that once the audition is over, we have no more control over the outcome and should let go of specific expectations. It becomes essential to become our own best friends instead of our own worst enemy.

This book is here to help you, to befriend you and raise you so that you feel empowered to reach your goals. However, the person primarily responsible for your growth and success is you. The most useful thing I have learnt throughout my career is that you must learn to be your own companion, even better, your own best friend. You need to become your biggest fan, your most loyal friend, your most enjoyable friend because this industry can often feel very lonely and judgemental. You must learn to love and forgive yourself, and to understand that if you did the work, put in the effort, and enjoyed the process, everything else is out of your hands. Sometimes, the role is just not the right fit for you. The director may have envisioned someone a little taller, rougher, or grumpier. Accept that you cannot control these factors, and whilst it may be disappointing, you have gained another learning experience.

Every audition allows us to learn and grow in our craft. We may have practised an accent, gained confidence, explored an unusual role, or nailed a highly emotional scene. There is always something to learn from each experience. It is not a waste of time or energy. And remember that not getting a particular role doesn't mean you didn't leave an impression. Perhaps you will be considered for another audition in the future. The point is that every experience helps you grow as both an actor and an individual. With a compassionate outlook towards yourself, you can become not only a successful actor but a happy one.

Having a positive mindset and outlook on life is equally important. Those who maintain a positive attitude are more productive, energetic, and accomplish more overall. How can you stay positive in the face of a series of rejections? When I began acting, I wrote an audition journal to log my thoughts, feelings, and learnings. This journal was so useful to me because for the first two years of acting, I never felt like I lost at an audition. Of course I felt the disappointment of rejection, but the journal allowed me to realise there was always something to learn. The journey to your desired future may take some time, or it may not, but we must be okay with either outcome. We need to be prepared for the long haul and find ways to enjoy the ride. If you focus on enjoying the journey, then you can live in happiness now.

Write down your experiences and remember them as positive, even if they went horribly wrong, write down what you learnt and reframe the experience. By doing this, you associate the audition process and your work with a positive mindset rather than an anxious or negative one. Things are likely to go wrong at some point, whether it's in an audition or on a job, but it's how you handle and deal with those situations that truly matters. One of my students had an audition for a big television series, and she completely messed up. She forgot everything, got upset, and walked out. Once out of the room, though, something changed inside of her. She wasn't going to let this opportunity end this way. She walked straight back in and politely asked if she could have another go. She smashed it, and guess what? Yes, she landed the role. The point is, many people wouldn't have done that. Many would have left that audition, gone home, and cried into their pillow. How are you going to face moments of challenge? Are you going to attack or retreat?

Writing down your feelings and emotions is important, especially at the beginning of your journey. It took me some time to start enjoying the auditioning process, but I bloody love it now! Putting pen to paper helped me understand some concerns

I had and allowed me to break down some unwarranted fears that I held. Writing your feelings down allows you to understand yourself so much more. We must accept and acknowledge all our feelings, even the negative ones, rather than suppressing or denying ourselves. The key to moving past negative feelings is to release them, give them a voice, and listen to what they have to say. What are they trying to tell you? Listen, take action, and then let them go.

Journaling allowed me to log inspirational quotes, key thoughts, and learning curves. It enabled me to log my journey and remember exactly how it all started and how far I had come. One quote that I will leave you with from my journal is from Denzel Washington: "If you don't fail, you're not even trying". When I heard this, it felt like a breakthrough moment because up until that moment I had seen all the rejections and all the "no's" as failures not as things that were getting me closer to that "yes". It is only when we truly embrace failure that we can win. Rome wasn't built in a day, and neither was the lightbulb. Things can take time, and this is something that we often have no control over. I say this to my clients all the time, focus on what you can control and not what you can't control, this will make you feel empowered and proactive rather than reactive.

13. Gratitude

In moments of bleakness, one thing you can control is remembering all the wonderful things you have in your life and how far you have come. Gratitude is the biggest player in the game of state shifting. How can you be sad and angry when you are grateful? Gratitude lifts us as we consider all the things in our life that we are thankful for. We are lucky in so many ways to be able to do what we love for a living, to have the life that we have, and the freedom that we get.

Often, we only appreciate the things that we take for granted when they are taken away from us. When we are sick, we remember what it is like to wake up healthy in the mornings and vow to remember that each day (but in time, we forget). You are fortunate and privileged to be reading this book just as I am privileged to write it. What are the things you have to be grateful for in your life? What achievements have you made, both acting-related and non-acting-related? Who do you have in your life that offers you friendship, love, and support? How is your health on a day-to-day basis?

Whenever you feel down, reach for your journal, and write down all the things that you have to be grateful for. It doesn't need to be all about the big things that you have achieved or bought; there is more to life than cars and awards. For me, it is often the smaller things that bring true value to my life: that delicious cup of coffee, my family who bring me joy, that hug from my best mate, a walk in the park, the sunrise, the amazing breakfast I ate, my wonderful soft bed sheets, the roof over my head, and the fact that I am alive. It can be anything. Living without gratitude keeps us living in a victim mode, which only contributes to a pessimistic attitude about the world and everyone in it.

Pessimism will not aid you on your path to success. When you hold a pessimistic energy, that's usually what you will attract in return. Focusing on the negative and on what you don't have alters your mood, your motivation, and your vibration. When you are feeling low, how easy is it to get motivated? Not very! The truth is, when we feel down many of our old limiting beliefs raise their head to taunt us, and in these moments, it is crucial that we have an awareness that those stories simply are not true. If we listen to the old limiting beliefs instead of challenging them we will look for any evidence out there to back them up and we will receive more of what we do not want. Don't indulge in the negative stories, try to see the side of the story you're not listening to, you know the one, the one filled with optimism and hope...

It takes energy and work, yes but I promise it is worth it. Like attracts like, and the energy you emit will come back to you. There is so much to be thankful for, even in the darkest times; there are always rays of hope and optimism shining somewhere. We just need to find them. Gratitude encourages positivity, which in turn influences every decision and action you make. When we are filled with gratitude, everything becomes possible, the glass is half-full, the world is conquerable, and life is more colourful. Our attitude shapes our success, and gratitude is heavily influential on this.

TASK

1. Purchase a journal. Use it to share your thoughts and feelings. It is so important we get to know ourselves and befriend ourselves. Do not judge yourself if you are down or are thinking negatively, instead show yourself kindness and compassion and put a strategy in place to reframe your thoughts and your energy so that they work for you.
2. Practice gratitude daily.

CONCLUSION

Thank you for embracing this journey with me. Thank you for your time, your purchase, and your dedication to learning. If you've reached the end, celebrate this win, you did it! I praise every single one of you for choosing to live your passion. I praise every single one of you for your creativity and light. I praise every single one of you for prioritising your mindset and your career. I hope that this book has helped you to build both an uncompromising technique and mindset. Now, it's up to you. The time is now to embrace your uniqueness, nurture your mindset, and become a happier actor in all areas of your life.

You are unique, you are special. No one can be a better version of you than yourself. The acting industry is both exciting and exhilarating. It is wonderful and challenging. It will make you cry and will make your heart fill with joy – sometimes at the same time. It can be unfair and cruel, uncertain and jarring, and your job is not just to perform well but to maintain professional relationships, a healthy mindset, and a healthy approach to the work. You must accept the industry as it is. It is useless romanticising it when we all know that it isn't all red carpets and champagne. We must expect the rejection, expect the silence, expect the fun, and expect the unexpected. It is safe to say that the acting industry can be both electrifying and intoxicating – if we allow it to be. However, if we can celebrate the highs but not expect them and reframe the "lows" so that they work for us not against us, surely we can sustain a happy and optimistic career instead of one rooted in anxiety and pessimism?

To accomplish this, you must delve deep into self-discovery. I encourage you to get to know yourself better than anyone so that you have the key to unlock your true potential. Get to know how you work, how you think, and how you act in accordance with your environment and emotions. Understand your triggers, your fears, and your motivators. This knowledge brings power. Power over your emotions and consequently power over your behaviour – which controls everything that you do. Practice self-awareness so that you can hear the fears that hold you back and unearth your limiting beliefs. Practice compassion so that you can understand your insecurities and release them. Practice reframing so that you can manage your expectations and do not surrender to stories that simply are not true. Practice self-love so that you enforce strong boundaries and take daily action to support your growth, career, and mind. Learn emotional regulation to become the master of you. Look for the light and stay true to yourself.

You are a courageous and powerful actor – I know this because you've reached the end of this book, and for that, I am truly grateful. If you sense that you're self-sabotaging, do something about it. If you feel that you lack confidence, do something about it. If you feel that others' opinions matter more to you than that of your own, do something about it. The tasks here in the book will help and guide you, but it's up to you to take action. Do not allow other people to control your self-worth; that power belongs to you alone.

I encourage all actors to work on their mindset, self-awareness, and technique throughout their careers. This is your responsibility, and with a strong commitment, you can have a happy and successful career. You cannot fail. Seek guidance when necessary, whether through a life coach, personal trainer, book, training programme, or acting tutor. Journal and document your progress, thoughts, emotions, and daily check-ins. Always remember to enjoy the process and the learning that comes along the way.

NOW, HERE'S MY LAST PIECE OF ADVICE FOR THOSE WHO WISH TO HEAR IT:

Embrace fear.

Educate yourself.

Challenge your thoughts.

Challenge your beliefs.

Create a vision.

Make affirmations.

Act in accordance with your values.

Act in accordance with the person you want to be.

Practice compassion to both yourself and others.

Get to know yourself.

Understand any resistance you may feel.

Accept the necessary sacrifices you need to make to reach your goal.

Journal your thoughts and feelings.

Avoid judging your feelings.

Reframe your thoughts to serve you.

Meditate daily.

Move your body daily.

Check in with yourself.

Talk.

Eat a healthy diet.

Respect yourself.

Be kind to yourself.

Practice your technique.

Play.

Be grateful.

Remember who and what really matters.

Show empathy.

Have courage.

Maintain faith.

Learn how to emotionally regulate.

Give back and serve others – it feels good.

Let go of outcomes.

Collaborate.

Have fun.

Be inspired.

Show up 100 percent.

Be less impressed by others.

Be more impressed by yourself.

Take ACTION.

Be your own best friend.

You are a bundle of bright, sparkling, burning energy. It's time for you to show the world your power. You've got this.

BIBLIOGRAPHY

Alfreds, Mike. *Different Every Night:* Freeing the Actor. Nick Hern Books, 2014.

Barr, Tony, and Eric Stephan Kline. *Acting for the Camera.* Lst ed., rev. Ed, Harper Perennial, 1997.

Bartow, Arthur. *Handbook of Acting Techniques.* Nick Hern, 2008.

Bishop, Gary John. *Unf*ck Yourself: Get out of Your Head and into Your Life.* Yellow Kite, 2018.

Caldarone, M, Lloyd-Williams. Actions: *The Actors' Thesaurus.* Nick Hern, 2004.

Dispenza, Dr Joe. Becoming Supernatural: *How Common People Are Doing the Uncommon.* Hay House UK LTD, 2019.

Dispenza, Joe. *Breaking the Habit of Being Yourself:* How to Lose Your Mind and Create a New One. 1st ed, Hay House, 2012.

Esper, William, and Damon DiMarco. *The Actor's Art and Craft: William Esper Teaches the Meisner Technique.* Anchor Books, 2008.

Gawdat, Mo. Solve for *Happy: Engineer Your Path to Joy.* Bluebird, 2017.

Goleman, Daniel. *Emotional Intelligence.* Bantam Books, 1995.

Hagen, Uta. *A Challenge for the Actor.* Scribner's; Maxwell Mac-millan Canada: Maxwell Macmillan International, 1991.

Hagen, Uta. *Respect for Acting.* John Wiley & Sons, Inc., Hoboken, 2009.

Hoobyar, Tom, et al. NLP: *The Essential Guide to Neuro-Linguistic Programming*. 1st ed, William Morrow, 2013.

Johnstone, Keith. *Impro for Storytellers: Theatresports and the Art of Making Things Happen*. Faber and Faber, 1999.

Kennedy, Russell. Anxiety Rx: *A New Prescription for Anxiety Relief from the Doctor Who Created It*. Awaken Village Press, 2020.

McConaughey, Matthew. *Greenlights*. Headline, 2023.

Merlin, Bella. *The Complete Stanislavsky Toolkit. Rev. ed.*, Nick Hern Books, 2014.

Moseley, N. *Actioning and How To Do It*. Nick Hern Books, 2016.

Murphy, Joseph. *The Power of Your Subconscious Mind*. Edited by Arthur R. Pell, Simon & Schuster, 2018.

Peters, Steve. *The Chimp Paradox*. Vermilion, 2020.

Robbins, Anthony. *Awaken the Giant within: How to Take Immediate Control of Your Mental, Emotional, Physical and Financial Destiny*. Pocket, 2001.

Stahl, Stefanie. *The Child In You: The Breakthrough Method for Bringing Out Your Authentic Self*. Penguin, 2021.

Stanislavski, Konstantin Sergeevič, and Elizabeth Reynolds Hapgood. *An Actor Prepares*. Bloomsbury, 2013.

Sparks, Nicholas. *The Notebook. Little, Brown and Company*, 1998.

Tolle, Eckhart. *The Power of Now: A Guide to Spiritual Enlightenment*. Hachette Australia, 2004.

Vitale, Joe. *The Abundance Paradigm: Moving from the Law of Attraction to the Law of Creation*. G&D Media, 2022.

www.ingramcontent.com/pod-product-compliance
Lightning Source LLC
Chambersburg PA
CBHW052054110526
44591CB00013B/2201